Questionnaire Research

A Practical Guide

Second Edition

Mildred L. Patten

Pyrczak Publishing

P.O. Box 39731 • Los Angeles, CA 90039

Editorial assistance provided by Sharon Young, Elaine Fuess, Brenda Koplin, and Cheryl Alcorn.

Cover design by Robert Kibler and Larry Nichols.

Printed in the United States of America.

ISBN 1-884585-32-9

Contents

Notes:

Introduction

This book provides step-by-step guidance on how to write and use questionnaires in research.

The distinctive features of this book are:

- The division of each chapter into easy-to-follow guidelines.

- The inclusion of large numbers of examples that illustrate the guidelines.

- An emphasis on writing questionnaire items. Four chapters are devoted to this topic. This emphasis is appropriate because properly constructed items are essential to sound questionnaire research.

- Detailed information on how to conduct item tryouts and an item analysis. Properly used, these techniques increase the validity of questionnaires.

- Practical advice on basic methods of statistical analysis—advice that tells you specifically when and how to use each statistical technique.

- End-of-chapter exercises that give you a chance to apply what you have learned.

Why do you need to know how to conduct questionnaire research? Because . . .

- Many of you will be expected to conduct questionnaire research as a class project. In addition, some of you may need to collect data using a questionnaire for a thesis or dissertation.

- Most of you will either be writing and administering questionnaires on the job or reading the results of questionnaire research conducted by your employer. Successful businesses, institutions, and government agencies today routinely gather information using questionnaires.

- All of you will be consuming questionnaire research in your everyday lives. Knowing how to conduct questionnaire research will make you a better consumer of the research reported in the mass media.

So why a whole book on this topic? Can't anyone who can write reasonably well assemble a set of questions and administer them to respondents? Take a peek inside this book. I think you'll be surprised by how much there is to learn. At the same time, I hope you find your learning experience interesting and enjoyable.

A Note on Statistics

The short chapters on statistics in this book will allow you to get started analyzing and interpreting your questionnaire research data. To the extent possible, I have minimized statistical theory and tried to provide guidelines that even those without prior statistical training can follow.

Those of you who have already taken a statistics course can use the chapters on statistics in this book as a review of basic concepts and procedures. The rest of you should consider taking a statistics course in which you will learn about more advanced options for analyzing data and how to use computers to perform the calculations.

New to the Second Edition

Although minor adjustments have been made throughout the book, the Second Edition remains essentially the same as the First Edition except for the addition of three new appendices: D, E, and F.

Appendix D presents a *first draft* questionnaire designed to measure attitudes toward statistics, and Appendix E presents one for a campus bookstore evaluation. Because they are first drafts, they are *not* intended to be models of excellence. Instead, they are included as stimulus material for classroom discussions. As you work through Chapters 1–5 and Chapter 7, you should refer repeatedly to these appendices, make notes on both strong and weak features of each questionnaire, and bring your notes to class for discussion.

Appendix F presents the questions on race/ethnicity posed in the 2000 Census. While they may be subject to legitimate criticism by some, the Census Bureau had expert advice on the wording of the questions, and they are worth your consideration while you write questions on this topic.

Acknowledgments

Dr. Richard Rasor of American River College and Dr. Robert Morman of California State University, Los Angeles provided many helpful comments on the first draft of this book. Their assistance is greatly appreciated. Errors and omissions, of course, remain the responsibility of the author.

Mildred L. Patten

Chapter 1

Planning Questionnaire Research

This chapter describes guidelines for planning questionnaire research. In subsequent chapters, we will consider how to write questionnaire items, refine them through tryouts, assemble them, administer them to respondents, analyze the responses, and write reports of the findings.

Guideline 1.1 Consider the advantages and disadvantages of using questionnaires.

All methods of collecting data have strengths and weaknesses. You should consider those unique to questionnaires before deciding to undertake questionnaire research.

In the following discussion of the advantages and disadvantages of written questionnaires, we will briefly compare questionnaires with two major alternatives for collecting data:

- Structured telephone interviews in which all respondents are asked the same questions—usually short-answer or multiple-choice questions.
- In-depth, semistructured personal interviews in which interviewers have some questions they ask all respondents but may also follow up with additional questions constructed on the spot to take advantage of leads, obtain additional details, and so on.

Major Advantages of Using Questionnaires in Research

Questionnaires provide an efficient way to collect data. For example, if school administrators want to know which illegal drugs high school seniors use and how often they use them, they can construct a questionnaire that may be administered simultaneously to hundreds of seniors throughout their school district. In contrast, telephone interviews and personal interviews are usually considerably less efficient since both alternatives require one-on-one data collection.

Questionnaires yield responses that usually are easy to tabulate or score, and the resulting data are easy to analyze—especially if the questionnaires contain mainly items with choices to be checked, which is recommended in this book. Since telephone interviews usually are based on the same types of questions as those used in questionnaires, they are about as easy to tabulate as questionnaires. In contrast, semistructured personal interviews will produce narrative material—

sometimes a tremendous amount of such material — which can be difficult and time-consuming to summarize and interpret.

Because questionnaires can be administered anonymously, they are useful for collecting information on sensitive matters or even illegal activities. Knowing that their responses are anonymous encourages respondents to be truthful. In contrast, responses to telephone interviews and personal interviews are inherently *not* anonymous. Of course, the interviewers can assure respondents that their responses will remain confidential, but many respondents may be skeptical. Note that researchers conducting personal interviews may be able to build rapport with respondents, leading them to develop a sense of trust and be open in their responses. This is far from assured, however, even if professional interviewers conduct the interviews.

Questionnaire research is economical. If you are conducting the research without paid assistants, the only major expenses will be for duplication and, if the questionnaires are mailed to the respondents, postage. Mailing questionnaires allows you to economically contact many subjects who are geographically distant from you. Telephone interviews also allow you to easily contact respondents who are geographically distant, but the interviews must be conducted one at a time, leading to personnel costs if assistants must be hired. Also, there will be long-distance telephone charges if respondents are located at a distance. One-on-one personal interviews are the most expensive, especially if the interviewers must travel to reach the respondents.

Major Disadvantages of Using Questionnaires in Research

The first major disadvantage of questionnaires is that the response rate is often low — especially if the questionnaires are mailed to potential respondents who do not personally know the researcher.[1] This is an acute problem since considerable research indicates that nonrespondents tend to be less well educated and from lower socioeconomic status groups than respondents. Thus, failure of all those selected to respond is presumed to bias the results of a survey conducted with mailed questionnaires. Generally, you can expect higher response rates when contacting potential respondents by telephone and even higher response rates when contacting them in person for personal interviews. Put another way, people find it easier to discard a questionnaire they regard as impersonal than to say, "No, I won't answer your questions" to someone who has contacted them personally by phone or in person.

Mailed questionnaires do not always lead to low response rates. For example, a college president might send questionnaires through the campus mail to members of the faculty and receive a very high rate of return. In addition, questionnaires are not always mailed. For instance, a workshop leader might distribute questionnaires to participants in a workshop. The participants are likely

---

[1] Techniques for increasing the response rate to mailed questionnaires are discussed in Chapter 7.

to complete them because time has been allotted during the workshop for this activity.

The second major disadvantage of questionnaires stems from the fact that they usually work best when they contain objective items (that is, items to which the responses can be scored objectively, such as items with choices that respondents check and short-answer items that require very limited responses, such as responses to the question, "What is your age?"). Because of the objective form of the items on questionnaires, respondents tend to move through them quickly, giving the responses that first come to mind. Thus, questionnaires usually provide only a snapshot rather than a rich, in-depth picture of an area of concern. For example, while a questionnaire can be used to determine which illegal drugs students use, how often they use them, why they started using them, and so on, questionnaire data will not reveal the rich context and texture that in-depth interviews can provide. A professional interviewer conducting a semistructured personal interview may be able to establish rapport with respondents, get them to explore their feelings, and spend time thinking about issues related to their drug use that they may not have seriously considered before. In addition, an interviewer can easily follow up on interesting leads, change the focus of the interviews as needed, and take note of respondents' nonverbal communications. Since telephone interviews work best when the questions require only limited responses, they are not noticeably superior to questionnaires with respect to obtaining in-depth information.

Another disadvantage of questionnaires is that some respondents do not provide accurate responses. For example, many people are swayed by *social desirability*. That is, they tend to give answers that they think are socially acceptable — even if they are not fully accurate. Although making the responses anonymous will reduce the effects of social desirability, the need for approval and the desire to seek it is so strong in some people that they will give socially desirable answers even when their responses are anonymous. Unfortunately, data collected by means of the other two alternatives — telephone interviews and personal interviews — are also subject to social desirability, and may be even more so since the respondents are not anonymous to the interviewers.

Guideline 1.2   Prepare written objectives for the research.

The first step in conducting questionnaire research is to prepare a written list of specific objectives for the research. The more specific you can be, the more likely it is that you will avoid getting off track while writing your questionnaire. Example 1.2.1 shows an objective that is too broad to provide direct guidance in writing questionnaire items. The Improved Version of Example 1.2.1 is much more specific. The elements listed in the improved version provide specific guidance for item writing—one or more items should be written for each element.

Example 1.2.1

Objective: To explore customers' satisfaction with their service visit to the repair shop of an automobile dealer.

Improved Version of Example 1.2.1

Objective: To determine customers' satisfaction with their service visit to the repair shop of an automobile dealer in terms of:
A. how long they waited before being greeted by customer service
B. the availability of parts for the repairs
C. correctly fixing the automobile
D. amount of time taken to fix the automobile
E. getting a status report while waiting for repairs
F. having the repairs completed when promised
G. getting an explanation of the work performed
H. the cost of the repairs

Example 1.2.2 shows another objective for questionnaire research that is insufficiently specific. Compare it with the improved version.

Example 1.2.2

Objective: To explore parents' reactions to the new requirement that their children wear uniforms to school.

Improved Version of Example 1.2.2

Objective: To determine parents' reactions to the new requirement that their children wear uniforms to school in terms of:
A. cost of uniforms
B. potential for reducing gang-related activities
C. potential for improving discipline in the classroom
D. potential for reducing competition for status among children
E. potential for improving learning in the classroom
F. potential for reducing individuality and individual expression
G. materials for uniforms (cotton, synthetics, blends)
H. uniform colors
I. overall degree of support for mandatory uniforms

Sometimes the objective of questionnaire research is to test a hypothesis. Example 1.2.3 shows such an objective. To test the hypothesis, questionnaire items will need to be written for each of the elements listed as defining "better socialization."

Example 1.2.3

Objective: To test the hypothesis that foster care adolescents in small group homes will report better socialization with their peers than those residing in large group homes. Better socialization is defined as:

A. having more close friends
B. confiding more in friends
C. spending more time with friends
D. engaging in more small group activities with peers
E. engaging in more team sports with peers
F. having fewer arguments with peers
G. having fewer fights with peers
H. expressing more concern about the welfare of peers
I. expressing a greater interest in social activities with peers than engaging in activities in isolation

Guideline 1.3   Have your objectives reviewed by others.

Take advantage of the insights of others by asking them if your objectives are realistic, whether any seem trivial or unnecessary, and whether any important ones have been omitted.

Note that when you write items, you should write only those that help you achieve your written objectives. It's important to resist the temptation to ask additional questions out of simple curiosity. Superfluous items will make your questionnaire lose its cohesiveness and make respondents wonder what your real objectives are. In addition, such questions will make your questionnaire longer, which may reduce the response rate. Thus, once you have established objectives for your research, it is important to stick closely to them when writing questionnaire items. In light of this, the need to refine your objectives by having them reviewed is obvious.

Guideline 1.4   Review the literature related to the objectives.

The purpose of reviewing literature early in a research project is to learn from the work of others. By reviewing related literature, you often will learn how others formulated their objectives, approached particular problems in conducting the research, and how successful they were in collecting the information they needed. In addition, you will sometimes find that others have already spent considerable time and effort developing a questionnaire that you can use (or modify for use) in your study. Furthermore, when you write a report on your study, you often will want to include a review of the literature on your topic. Guidelines for writing research reports are presented in Chapter 13.

For individuals in the social and behavioral sciences, literature can be located electronically (via computer) from three major sources: (1) *ERIC*, which contains abstracts to articles in education found in more than 600 journals going back to 1966 as well as unpublished documents such as convention papers and government reports; (2) *PsycLIT*, which contains the print version of *Psychological Abstracts* containing abstracts of journal articles published since 1974; and (3) *Sociofile*, which contains the print versions of *Sociological Abstracts* and *Social Planning/Policy & Development Abstracts* covering journal articles published in more than 1,600 journals.

Guideline 1.5   Determine the feasibility of administering your questionnaire to the population of interest.

This guideline suggests that you try to determine early in your research planning whether you will be able to gain access to the population of interest in order to administer your questionnaire.[2] For example, if you hope to administer questionnaires to public school children, contact the appropriate school administrators as soon as you have written your objectives. Share your objectives with them to determine whether they are willing to give you access to the children. Don't be surprised, however, if they withhold final approval until you provide them with a copy of the questionnaire you plan to use. They may also wish to see your "informed consent" form, which is discussed in Chapter 7.

Guideline 1.6   Prepare a timeline.

Your timeline can be as simple as showing what you plan to accomplish each week or month. Example 1.6.1 shows a timeline that includes the major steps in conducting questionnaire research prepared by someone who plans to spend up to 20 hours per week working on the research project.

Example 1.6.1

Timeline for a Questionnaire Research Project:

Week 1	Prepare a written draft of the research objectives. Begin literature review.
Weeks 2-3	Have objectives reviewed by others. Continue literature review.
Week 4	Revise objectives in light of reviews. Track down hard-to-locate literature.
Weeks 5-6	Prepare draft of literature review. Revise objectives in light of the literature review.
Week 7	Prepare a draft of the questionnaire items.

---

[2] Very often, questionnaires are administered to only a sample from a population. Methods of sampling are discussed in Chapter 8.

Weeks 8-9	Have the questionnaire items reviewed by others. Obtain the mailing list. Order envelopes. Have the literature review critiqued by others.
Week 10	Revise the items and literature review in light of the reviewers' comments.
Weeks 11-12	Try out the items with respondents who will not be in the main study.
Week 13	Revise items in light of the tryouts. Arrange items in the questionnaire.
Weeks 14-15	Prepare cover letter and have it reviewed by others. Have letter and questionnaire duplicated.
Week 16	Mail questionnaire.
Week 17	Begin tabulating results as questionnaires are received.
Week 18	Continue tabulating results.
Week 19	Mail follow-up questionnaires to nonrespondents.
Week 20	Continue tabulating results.
Week 21	Begin writing a report of the research.
Week 22	Finish tabulating results and analyze data.
Weeks 23-24	Complete first draft of the research report.
Weeks 25-26	Have the first draft of the research report reviewed by others.
Week 27	Revise the first draft in light of the review. Have report proofread.
Week 28	Duplicate and disseminate the report.

Note that the timeline for your research may vary considerably from the one in the example, depending on your work habits and the complexity of your topic and questionnaire. The only firm principle in planning a timeline is to be generous in the allotment of time—*most research projects take much longer than the researchers initially anticipated*. Be especially generous in allotting time for the review of your objectives and items by others. Pressed by other high-priority obligations, your reviewers may not be able to consider your materials immediately.

Exercise for Chapter 1

1. Of the three methods for collecting data discussed in this chapter, which one is usually the most efficient?

2. Of the three methods for collecting data discussed in this chapter, which one allows for the collection of anonymous responses?

3. Why is the potentially low rate of response to a mailed questionnaire an acute problem?

4. Briefly describe the problem of *social desirability*.

5. Why is it recommended that literature be reviewed early in a research project?

6. What are the disadvantages of including superfluous items in a questionnaire? That is, why should you avoid writing items that go beyond your research objectives?

7. According to the chapter, what is the "only firm guideline in planning a timeline" for questionnaire research?

8. Select a topic of interest to you, and write specific objectives that might guide you in the development of a questionnaire to explore that topic.

Chapter 2

Writing Items to Collect Factual Information

As you know from Chapter 1, each item in a questionnaire should relate to a specific objective of your research. You will not be able to achieve your objectives, however, unless your items are well crafted. Poorly written items will confuse, frustrate, and turn off your respondents. In this chapter, we will consider 14 guidelines that will help you avoid major mistakes when writing items to collect factual information. In Chapter 3, we will consider how to write items to collect demographic information (that is, background information such as age and ethnicity). Although demographic questions also ask for factual information, they are considered in more detail in a separate chapter because they sometimes pose special problems for item writers.

Guideline 2.1   Consider asking respondents to recall behavior only over a limited, recent time period.

In Example 2.1.1, respondents are asked to indicate the total number of hours they have used various Internet services. Those who have used the Internet extensively over a long period probably will be unable to give accurate estimates. It is more reasonable to ask for the number of hours over a one-week period, as is done in the Improved Version of Example 2.1.1.

Example 2.1.1

Have you ever used:

E-mail?	☐ No	☐ Yes	If yes, total number of hours used: _____
Newsgroups?	☐ No	☐ Yes	If yes, total number of hours used: _____
Internet phone?	☐ No	☐ Yes	If yes, total number of hours used: _____

Improved Version of Example 2.1.1

Have you ever used:

E-mail?	☐ No	☐ Yes	If yes, number of hours used last week: _____
Newsgroups?	☐ No	☐ Yes	If yes, number of hours used last week: _____
Internet phone?	☐ No	☐ Yes	If yes, number of hours used last week: _____

Of course, some respondents may have had an unusual week, leading them to use these Internet services more or less often than usual, creating errors if the researcher wishes to estimate typical usage. It is important to note, however, that these errors will *wash each other out* in the averages across large numbers of respondents. For example, for each respondent who used e-mail less often than usual (for example, because she was on vacation), there is probably another who used it more often than usual (for example, because he was given a special assignment at work requiring extensive use of e-mail).

The suitability of a time period depends on the maturity of the respondents and the likelihood that they can recall the information solicited. For example, if a teacher is studying how much time fourth graders spend watching TV, a week may be too long for accurate recall by students at this grade level. By asking only how much TV they watched the previous day, the teacher may obtain more accurate information. To control for variations from day to day in the appeal of programming to children, the teacher might ask this question several times—each time on a different day of the week.

Some life events are so salient that almost everyone will be able to recall them even if they occurred in the distant past. Thus, it is acceptable to ask questions such as, "Were you ever married?" and "Have you ever served in the armed forces?"

Note that your objectives may require you to ask about potentially distant behavior even if the events are not salient. If you are studying smoking behavior, you may need to ask adults, "At what age did you first try smoking cigarettes?" even though some of them might not be able to recall the answer accurately. When there is doubt about respondents' ability to accurately recall a past event, a companion question asking them to rate their confidence in the answer may provide useful information. Such a companion question is shown in Example 2.1.2.

Example 2.1.2

1. At what age did you first try smoking cigarettes? _____
   → How confident are you in the accuracy of your answer to question 1?
      A. Very confident   B. Moderately confident
      C. Somewhat confident   D. Not at all confident

Guideline 2.2   Use "always" and "never" with caution.

Few things in life are "never" or "always." Thus, it's usually better to use "almost never" and "almost always." Consider the items in a marriage questionnaire in Example 2.2.1. The choices "never" and "always" are likely to be dead choices, with few respondents selecting them—assuming that they interpret the choices literally.

Example 2.2.1

Speaks to me in a loving voice.
O Never O Sometimes O Often O Always

Finds fault with me.
O Never O Sometimes O Often O Always

Of course, for some questions, "Never" and "Always" may be appropriate choices. For example, "Never" will be an appropriate choice for many respondents to the question in Example 2.2.2. Note that in this example "Always" is not used since it is not possible for someone to always smoke marijuana in a given month.

Example 2.2.2

How often have you smoked marijuana in the past month?
O Never O Sometimes O Often O Very often

The choices for Example 2.2.2 could present specific numbers of times. For example, the item writer could keep the choice "never" and replace "sometimes" with "1 to 6 times," replace "often" with "7 to 12 times," and "very often" with "13 or more times."

Guideline 2.3   Avoid using negatives in statements.

Negatives are easily overlooked and can cause confusion. Consider Example 2.3.1, which appeared in a questionnaire on the reactions to the death of a loved one.

Example 2.3.1

I can't stop thinking about how the death occurred.
O Very rarely O Rarely O Sometimes O Often O Very often

It's easy to get confused when responding to the item in the example because of the negative. For example, a person who marks "very rarely" is saying:

I very rarely can't stop thinking about how the death occurred.

In contrast, someone who marks "very often" is saying:

I very often can't stop thinking about how the death occurred.

Confusing isn't it? Stating the concept in the positive solves the problem, as illustrated in the Improved Version of Example 2.3.1.

Improved Version of Example 2.3.1

I keep thinking about how the death occurred.
   ○ Very rarely   ○ Rarely   ○ Sometimes   ○ Often   ○ Very often

If you feel you must use a negative in an item, underline, boldface, or italicize it to draw respondents' attention to it.

Guideline 2.4   Each item should ask only a single question.

The item in Example 2.4.1 concerns two points: employment status and student status. What should a respondent mark if she is retired and is a full-time student? Should she mark two choices? What should a respondent mark if he is a part-time student and employed part-time? Breaking the question up into two questions, as was done in the Improved Version of Example 2.4.1, solves these problems.

Example 2.4.1

Occupational status:
- ☐   Full-time employment
- ☐   Full-time student
- ☐   Part-time student
- ☐   Unemployed
- ☐   Retired

Improved Version of Example 2.4.1

Occupational status:
- ☐   Full-time employment
- ☐   Part-time employment
- ☐   Unemployed
- ☐   Retired

Student status:
- ☐   Full-time student
- ☐   Part-time student
- ☐   Not a student

Asking more than one question in a single item is a mistake frequently committed by novice item writers, so let's consider a couple of other examples. Example 2.4.2 is asking three things: (1) how many tasks are performed, (2) the level of skill required to complete the tasks, and (3) the amount of effort required. How should a brain surgeon who performs basically one task that requires much skill and effort respond? Clearly, this item should be broken into three separate ones.

Example 2.4.2

Does your job challenge your abilities and require you to perform a variety of tasks?
O I perform basically one task with very little skill and effort required.
O I perform a fair number of different tasks, which require some skill and effort.
O I perform a very wide range of tasks involving a high degree of skill and effort.

The item in Example 2.4.3 asks two questions: (1) Do you know anyone who is HIV+? and (2) Are you HIV+? They should be stated as separate items.

Example 2.4.3

Do you know anyone who is HIV+?
☐ Yes   ☐ No   ☐ I am HIV+

Guideline 2.5   Make the choices for an item exhaustive.

The choices in Example 2.5.1 are not exhaustive because they do not allow for all possibilities. What about someone who listens to music while at work? The problem is easily solved by adding the choice "Other," with a space to write in the other choice, as illustrated in the improved version.

Example 2.5.1

What activities do you engage in while listening to music? (Check all that apply.)
O Studying   O Driving   O Eating   O Exercising   O Socializing

Improved Version of Example 2.5.1

What activities do you engage in while listening to music? (Check all that apply.)
O Studying   O Driving   O Eating   O Exercising   O Socializing
O Other. Please specify: _____

Note that "Other" should be used for choices that you believe will be relatively rare. If you think that many people listen to music while working, "Working" should be included as one of the choices. "Other" should still be included because it is difficult to predict in advance all the activities people might engage in while listening to music.

Guideline 2.6   Spell out acronyms and define difficult-to-understand terms.

A university administrator recently wrote a questionnaire for distribution to students. In it, there were numerous references to IHEs. When the questionnaire was reviewed by members of the faculty before it was mailed, several of them suggested that the acronym, "IHE," be spelled out—at least the first time it was used. The administrator responded that this was unnecessary because "all students know what an IHE is." Do you? (None of my students did.) Obviously, IHE (Institution of Higher Education) should have been spelled out. But how could an intelligent person make such a mistake? The administrator had used the acronym so often that it seemed like an everyday term to him. How can you avoid making this mistake? A partial solution is to ask yourself whether an acronym or technical term is one you learned in an advanced course or in a specialized occupation. If the answer is "Yes," you need to spell out the acronym or define the technical term.

In Example 2.6.1, there is a list of symptoms included in a health questionnaire. Notice that one of the symptoms is defined in parentheses. It would be a good idea if the item writer also defined "malaise," since this is a word that we don't often hear people use in everyday conversations. Suspicious words can be checked against graded word lists. One of the best is Dale and O'Rourke's *The Living Word Vocabulary*.[1] It indicates that only 57% of college freshmen know the meaning of the word "malaise."

Example 2.6.1

Rate each of the following <u>nonallergy</u> symptoms you had during the <u>last month</u>.

Headache	O No	O Yes	If yes:	O mild	O moderate	O severe
Coughing	O No	O Yes	If yes:	O mild	O moderate	O severe
Nonallergy nasal obstruction (stuffy nose)	O No	O Yes	If yes:	O mild	O moderate	O severe
Malaise	O No	O Yes	If yes:	O mild	O moderate	O severe
Fever	O No	O Yes	If yes:	O mild	O moderate	O severe

It might be desirable to omit the term "Nonallergy nasal obstruction" and just use "Stuffy nose" unless some of the respondents are health care professionals who might object to the informality of the term.

---

[1] Dale, E. and O'Rourke, J. (1976). *The Living Word Vocabulary*. Elgin, IL: Dome, Inc.

Guideline 2.7   Underline, italicize, or use bold print to draw respondents' attention to important terms.

In Example 2.6.1 above, the terms *nonallergy* and *last month* are underlined. Be careful not to overdo it, however. Too many underlined, italicized, and boldfaced words may distract respondents from the few key terms that are really important to notice.

Guideline 2.8   Use "Don't know" sparingly as a choice.

"Don't know" should be provided as a choice only when it is reasonable to expect that some respondents really won't know the answer to an item. Providing it as a choice in items that all respondents probably know the answers to invites them to avoid answering the items by responding "Don't know." Keep in mind that respondents often need to ponder a moment to answer an item. The "Don't know" option provides them with a lazy way out.

In Example 2.8.1, "Don't know" is provided as a choice for the first two questions because some respondents truly may not know the answer. Although it's a judgment call, it seems likely that all will know their own birth order, so "Don't know" probably is not needed in the third item.[2]

Example 2.8.1

For the following questions, write numbers in the boxes. For example, if your mother is the second-born child out of three children, this should be your response to the first item:

2 │ out of │ 3 │ child(ren)   ○ Don't know

1. My mother's birth order is:

□ out of □ child(ren)   ○ Don't know

2. My father's birth order is:

□ out of □ child(ren)   ○ Don't know

3. My birth order is:

□ out of □ child(ren)

---

[2] Note that when using an unusual item format, such as the one in Example 2.8.1, it is a good idea to provide specific instructions and a sample response.

Guideline 2.9   Be specific in your requests for information.

Of course you know to be specific in your requests for information, but it is easy to slip up. Because you are thoroughly familiar with the objectives for your survey, it's easy to forget that your respondents are not.

In Example 2.9.1, the item writer failed to indicate the types of writing activities respondents are to consider. Should respondents consider writing grocery lists? Writing phone messages? Writing essays for school? Writing personal letters? Writing a novel? The types of writing activities could be indicated in the instructions for the questionnaire if there will be many items on a specific type of writing or in individual items if different items will deal with different types of writing.

Example 2.9.1

On average, how many times do you write during the week? (Circle one.)
☐ 0-3 times   ☐ 4-6 times   ☐ 7-9 times   ☐ 10 or more times

Improved Version of Example 2.9.1

During an average week, how many times do you write short materials such as grocery lists, telephone messages, to-do notes, notes to family members, and so on?
☐ 0-3 times   ☐ 4-6 times   ☐ 7-9 times   ☐ 10 or more times

In Example 2.9.2, many respondents may assume that the term "interracial relationships" refers to dating or marriage, while others might wonder whether it includes friendships. Thus, "interracial relationships" should be replaced with a more specific term such as "interracial dating."

Example 2.9.2

How does your family feel about interracial relationships?
___ Strongly approve   ___ Approve   ___ Disapprove   ___ Strongly disapprove

Guideline 2.10   Carefully consider using "Yes" and "No" as choices.

"Yes" and "No" are obvious choices for many questions such as "Have you ever been pregnant?" For other questions, these choices may pose a dilemma for respondents. In Example 2.10.1, respondents who were aware of gang violence may find it difficult to decide whether it was "much." The improved version reduces this problem. In addition, the responses to it will provide more information than responses to the original item.

Example 2.10.1

Was there much gang violence at your high school? (Circle one.)
☐ Yes   ☐ No

Improved Version of Example 2.10.1[3]

How much gang violence were you aware of at your high school? (Circle one.)
☐ Much   ☐ Some   ☐ Very little   ☐ Almost none   ☐ None

Guideline 2.11   Avoid putting a blank in the middle of an item.

An item with a blank in the middle is distracting. Such items can almost always be satisfactorily rewritten without a blank. Consider Example 2.11.1 and its improved version.

Example 2.11.1

I spend _____ of my free time with my friends.
☐ Almost all   ☐ Most   ☐ Some   ☐ Little   ☐ Almost none

Improved Version of Example 2.11.1

How much of your free time do you spend with your friends?
☐ Almost all   ☐ Most   ☐ Some   ☐ Little   ☐ Almost none

Guideline 2.12   Make the choices mutually exclusive when only one choice is to be selected.

The question in Example 2.12.1 appeared in a questionnaire on Internet use. Which choice should a respondent mark if his or her best estimate is that they use personal e-mail 2 hours: "1–2 hours" or "2–3 hours"? The choices are not mutually exclusive because they overlap. Note that in the Improved Version of Example 2.12.1, the choices do not overlap. In addition, the mathematical symbols (< for "less than" and > for "greater than") have been replaced with words.

Example 2.12.1

On average, how much time do you spend each week using personal e-mail?
☐ Never use   ☐ < 1 hour   ☐ 1-2 hours   ☐ 2-3 hours   ☐ 3-4 hours   ☐ >4 hours

---

[3] The item writer might consider defining "gang violence" for respondents.

Improved Version of Example 2.12.1

On average, how much time do you spend each week using personal e-mail?
    ☐ Never use ☐ Less than 1 hour ☐ 1-2 hours
    ☐ 3-4 hours ☐ 5-6 hours ☐ More than 6 hours

Guideline 2.13   Use items that require ranking sparingly.

Having respondents rank the choices in a list occasionally may be appropriate, but it is important to notice that ranking indicates only the importance of a choice relative to other choices—not its absolute importance. To understand this point, consider Example 2.13.1 in which first-year teachers are asked to rank the problems they consider most important. An obvious problem with the item is that it presents a hodgepodge of possible problems. Suppose a teacher had serious discipline problems that he or she was unable to control *and* was seriously lacking in resources such as textbooks and computers. Asking the respondent to choose between the two in terms of importance is like asking him or her to compare apples and oranges. To get around this problem, the item writer should consider rewriting the item as a number of separate items with more homogeneous choices. One such item is shown in Example 2.13.2.

Example 2.13.1

Rank the importance of each of the following problems that you encountered during your first year of teaching. Write "1" next to the most important problem, "2" next to the next most important, and so on.
    _____ Discipline in the classroom
    _____ Uninvolved parents
    _____ Lack of support from school administrators
    _____ Lack of support from other teachers
    _____ Lack of resources such as textbooks, computers, and so on
    _____ Not understanding the goals of instruction
    _____ Low-achieving students
    _____ Other. Please specify: _____

Example 2.13.2[4]

Consider how much support you received from various people during your first year of teaching. Write "1" next to the most supportive person/people, write "2" next to the next most supportive, and so on.

_____ Parents
_____ Other teachers
_____ Principal
_____ Vice-principal
_____ School counselor(s)
_____ Family and friends
_____ Other. Please specify: _____

Although it will be easier for teachers to respond to the item in Example 2.13.2 than the one in Example 2.13.1, the item in Example 2.13.2 still has a major weakness: It will not tell us *how important* each choice is to the respondent. For example, consider Ms. Sharp, a first-year teacher who had good support from all those listed, but slightly more support from parents than from others on the list. She will give "Parents" a rank of 1. Consider another first-year teacher, Mr. Dull, who received very little support from anyone on the list; but of all the *unsupportive* ones, parents were the most supportive. He will also give "Parents" a rank of 1. Thus, two very different situations have led to a rank of 1 for parents. This type of problem can be avoided by having respondents indicate *how important* each source was without asking them to rank them, which is done in Example 2.13.3. In response to this item, Ms. Sharp can indicate that parents were "very supportive," while Mr. Dull can indicate that parents were "somewhat unsupportive." For most purposes, a series of items like the one in Example 2.13.3 will be more satisfactory than an item that requires choices to be ranked.

Example 2.13.3

How supportive were parents during your first year of teaching?
☐ Very supportive   ☐ Moderately supportive
☐ Somewhat unsupportive   ☐ Very unsupportive

Guideline 2.14 Use open-ended questions sparingly.

Consider the question in Example 2.14.1, which appeared in a questionnaire designed for college students. The item writer had in mind choices such as "freshman," "sophomore," and so on. To the item writer's dismay, some respondents wrote answers such as 14 (perhaps 12 years of public school plus two

---

[4] Although the item asks about "support," it will yield information about problems in first-year teaching since those choices with low ratings may indicate problem areas. Also, note that the item writer probably should describe what he or she means by "support."

years of college), 3 (perhaps a junior), and 6 (perhaps a student who has been attending part-time for six years). Clearly, these problems could have been avoided by providing choices.

Example 2.14.1

Year in school? _____

Open-ended questions may be appropriate when exploring a topic that is new (or is new to you). For example, when children were first required to wear uniforms by some public schools, there was virtually no literature on parents' reactions to uniforms. Rather than brainstorming a list of reasons why parents might favor or object to uniforms in order to write choices for items, an item writer might have conducted a pilot study in which parents were asked open-ended questions such as, "What do you like (if anything) about having your child/children wear uniforms to school?" and "What do you dislike (if anything) about having your child/children wear uniforms to school?" The responses of the parents to these open-ended questions in a pilot study could then be used as the basis for writing items with choices for use in the main study.

When considering the use of open-ended questions, keep in mind that many respondents will be turned off if they think that they have to write a well-crafted essay; it is too much like a test, is time-consuming, and can be threatening. Thus, you may want to indicate that respondents need only "jot down their ideas." If it is essential to ask a large number of open-ended questions (or even a few open-ended questions that each require extensive responses), you should consider using interviews instead of a questionnaire. Respondents tend to be less resistant to giving extensive responses in an interview setting than to writing essays in response to questions on a questionnaire.

Exercise for Chapter 2

Directions: For each of the following questionnaire items, briefly describe the flaw(s), if any. Your instructor may ask you to rewrite the items to eliminate the flaws.

1. With what political party do you identify? (Circle the letter of one choice.)
   A. Democrat   B. Republican   C. Independent   D. Conservative
   E. Liberal   F. Libertarian   G. Other

2. Have you ever used marijuana?
   ☐ Yes, more than 30 times and have in the past year
   ☐ Yes, fewer than 30 times and have in the past year
   ☐ Yes, more than 30 times but not in the past year
   ☐ Yes, fewer than 30 times but not in the past year
   ☐ No, never

3. I spend an average of _____ hours per week on the Internet.
   ☐ 0–2 ☐ 2–6 ☐ 6–10 ☐ 10–20 ☐ 20–40 ☐ 40+

4. Which characteristic of the Internet most appeals to you?
   ☐ Information ☐ Entertainment ☐ Shopping ☐ Communication

5. Which of the following reasons would keep you from riding a bicycle to work?
   (Check one or more.)
   ☐ Too far a trip ☐ Poor road conditions ☐ Fear of riding in traffic
   ☐ Topography ☐ Health-related reasons ☐ No shower at work
   ☐ Other. Please specify: _____

6. (*Note to students:* The following item was on a questionnaire about booking
   airline flights using the Internet.)
   Was this service easy to use?
   ☐ Yes   ☐ No

7. Do you think that Americans exercise enough and eat a wholesome diet?
   ☐ Yes   ☐ No

8. I enjoy chess because of the opportunities for friendships that it provides.
   ☐ Always ☐ Very often ☐ Often ☐ Sometimes ☐ Never

9. How many times have you felt pressured by the time limits for a classroom
   test?
   ☐ 0 to 10 ☐ 11 to 20 ☐ 21 to 30 ☐ 31 to 40 ☐ 41 or more

10. Have you performed a breast self-examination in the past 30 days?
☐ Yes ☐ No

11. Rank the reasons why you continue to smoke by giving a rank of 1 to the most important reason, a rank of 2 to the next most important reason, and so on.
_____ To maintain my weight
_____ To relieve stress
_____ To fit in with my friends
_____ To satisfy a craving for nicotine
_____ Other. Please specify: _____

12. Think of a time when you visited a doctor and felt satisfied with the office visit. What things made you feel satisfied?

13. Have you taken all the prescriptions *your doctor* gave you **exactly** as indicated on the label during the past year?
☐ Yes ☐ No

14. Including yourself, how many people are covered by your health plan?
☐ 1   ☐ 2–3   ☐ 3–4   ☐ 4+

15. How many times have you visited your primary care physician in the past month? Please write the number in the box below.

☐ (number of visits in past month)   If you don't know, check here: ☐

16. If the research objectives that you wrote for item 8 in the Exercise for Chapter 1 require you to collect factual information, write two or three items for those objectives.

Chapter 3

Writing Items to Collect Demographic Information

Researchers usually include demographic items on questionnaires. These request information on background characteristics such as age, race, ethnicity, religion, and so on. Sometimes this information is needed in order to fulfill a research objective. For example, a researcher will need to ask respondents to indicate their age if an objective is to determine whether older people are more likely to vote in general elections than younger people. In addition, demographic information is frequently collected so that researchers can get a mental picture of the respondents in order to convey this picture to their readers.

The principles in Chapter 2 should be applied while writing items about demographics. We are taking a closer look at these questions in a separate chapter for two reasons. First, they are used so frequently in questionnaires that you will almost certainly be writing some of them if you conduct questionnaire research. Second, many demographic items deal with sensitive topics. Unless they are carefully written, respondents may refuse to answer them.

Guideline 3.1   Ask about demographics sparingly.

There are two reasons for this guideline. First, asking a large number of demographic questions will make your questionnaire longer, and long questionnaires often get a lower response rate than short ones. Second, the more demographic questions you ask, the more likely it is that respondents may view the questionnaire as being intrusive into their privacy.

As a general rule, ask only about demographics that might be related to the topic being studied. For example, if you are studying the views of physicians on assisted suicide for terminally ill patients, you may want to collect information about their religious preferences since different religions oppose suicide to different degrees. On the other hand, if you are studying physicians' views on using the Internet to get up-to-date information on medical procedures, information on their religious preferences may be of little interest to you or your readers.

You may be able to reduce the need to collect demographic information by using information that is already available to you. For example, if you are distributing questionnaires only to high school seniors, it is probably unnecessary to ask their ages since it would be sufficient in your report to indicate that all respondents are high school seniors.

Guideline 3.2   Avoid invading the privacy of "others" with demographic items.

This guideline is especially important for those who work with minors. For example, it may be unethical to ask children on a questionnaire designed for research purposes about their parents' religion, income, and so on. Even if the minors will be responding anonymously, some parents may strongly object. If you really need the information, you should ask the parents directly or, at least, get their permission to ask their children. If you don't want to do that, you may be able to provide your readers with some related demographics. For example, you may know from school records what percentage of the schoolchildren who were surveyed qualified for the federal free lunch program. This percentage will shed some light on the income of the parents as a group—without the need to determine the incomes of individual families.

The issues of privacy and confidentiality will be explored more fully when we consider the use of informed consent procedures in Chapter 7.

Guideline 3.3   Consider providing ranges of values instead of asking for a precise value.

When responding to personal questions, such as questions about income, some individuals may be more willing to share a range of values with a researcher rather than a precise value. For example, Example 3.3.1 allows respondents to indicate their approximate income by asking them to select from choices that present ranges of income.

Providing a range of values has the added advantage of requiring less effort from respondents. If we simply asked, "What is your approximate household income before taxes?" without choices that present ranges of income, some respondents may feel the need to be relatively precise and consider wages, interest income, dividend income, and so on. Many respondents are unlikely to have this information readily at hand and, thus, may leave the question blank. Presenting ranges of income allows them to make rough approximations.

Example 3.3.1[1]

What is your approximate <u>household</u> income before taxes?
- ☐ Under $10,000
- ☐ $10,000 to less than $20,000
- ☐ $20,000 to less than $35,000
- ☐ $35,000 to less than $50,000
- ☐ $50,000 to less than $75,000
- ☐ $75,000 to less than $100,000
- ☐ $100,000 or more

Guideline 3.4   Carefully consider the ranges of values you present in an item.

You should attempt to develop ranges (see Guideline 3.3) that are likely to yield coarsely similar numbers of respondents in each range. This is desirable because, otherwise, you may lose important information. For example, if you have one range that inadvertently includes most respondents and other ranges that include very few, you will lose information about how most of the respondents differ from one another.

Following this guideline often may involve quite a bit of guesswork. At other times, you can get some hints from information that has already been gathered. For example, consider Example 3.4.1, which was written for a questionnaire on voting behavior. The first age category (18–24 years) covers seven years, while the second one (25–44) covers 20 years. This suggests a potential problem that can be confirmed by consulting U.S. Census figures, which indicate that there are approximately 25 million in the 18- to 24-year category, while there are 83 million in the 25- to 44-year category. To get better information, the second and third categories should probably be broken down into smaller ranges.[2]

Example 3.4.1

What is your age?
- ☐ 18–24 years
- ☐ 25–44 years
- ☐ 45–64 years
- ☐ 65 years and over

---

[1] If you do not think that all respondents will understand the term "household income," you might define it in the item.

[2] Incidentally, according to recent Census Bureau figures, there are about 51 million in the 45- to 64-year category, and about 31 million in the 65 years and over category.

Guideline 3.5   Use care when writing questions about race or ethnicity.

Many people are understandably sensitive to questions about race and ethnicity. Example 3.5.1, which was recently used by an insurance company in a questionnaire, illustrates some principles for writing such items.

Example 3.5.1

Which of the following best describes your racial or ethnic background?
Please check one.
☐ Asian
☐ Black/African American
☐ White/Caucasian
☐ Hispanic (may be any race)
☐ Native American
☐ Other. Please specify: _____

The first major problem when writing items such as the one in Example 3.5.1 is deciding what choices to provide. Providing alternative terms in choices such as was done with "Black/African American" and "White/Caucasian" usually is a good idea and might also have been done for the choice "Hispanic," with the inclusion of the term "Latino/a." The second major problem is whether to allow respondents to select only one choice, as was done in the example. This creates a problem for respondents who are of mixed ancestry. Allowing respondents to check more than one choice, on the other hand, creates problems in the interpretation of the data. For example, if 6% mark "Asian," the researcher will not know what percentage of them are of mixed ancestry (those who checked Asian as well as an additional choice or two) and what percentage are solely of Asian ancestry (those who checked only Asian). See Appendix F for the wording of such questions used in the 2000 Census.

You can avoid some of these problems by asking a question in open-ended form without choices. Of course, if you have a large number of respondents, this may greatly increase the time you need to spend tabulating the responses to the item.

Since satisfactory questions on race and ethnicity are difficult to write and may offend some of your respondents, ask such questions only if you feel it is important to do so.

Guideline 3.6   Use standard categories whenever possible.

Faulty demographic questions often result when novices write items off the tops of their heads instead of using the items written by professionals. For instance, Example 3.6.1 was written by a novice to determine marital status. Compare it with Example 3.6.2, which was used by the U.S. Census Bureau. Notice that the Census Bureau's version of the question is superior because it includes a category for those who are separated. Also, it makes clear the intended meaning of "Single," which is "Never married."

Example 3.6.1

Your Marital Status:
☐ Married
☐ Single
☐ Divorced
☐ Widowed

Example 3.6.2

Your Marital Status:
☐ Married
☐ Separated
☐ Widowed
☐ Divorced
☐ Never married

Example 3.6.3 shows another demographic question written by a novice item writer. Notice that it has several flaws including (1) not providing a choice for someone who has completed only some elementary school and (2) failing to indicate whether "College graduate" should include those who graduated from a two-year college. The Census Bureau's version, which is shown in Example 3.6.4, is clearer and more comprehensive.

Example 3.6.3

Highest level of education completed:
☐ Elementary
☐ Secondary
☐ Some college
☐ College graduate

Example 3.6.4

Highest level of education completed:
☐ Elementary (0 to 8 years)
☐ Some high school (1 to 3 years)
☐ High school graduate (4 years)
☐ Some college (1 to 3 years)
☐ College graduate (4 or more years)

For measuring demographic variables, it makes sense to examine questionnaires written by professional item writers and especially items developed by the United States Census Bureau. The Census Bureau's Home Page on the Internet is at "http://www.census.gov/" (type everything within quotation marks, but do *not* type the quotation marks). From there, you can explore a number of reports and get examples of ways to word demographic questions.

Guideline 3.7   Consider placing demographic questions at the end of the questionnaire.

Because many demographic questions may be regarded as personal or sensitive, it is usually best to place them near the end of a questionnaire. Having invested time and thought in answering the earlier questions, some respondents who mildly object to the personal nature of the demographic questions may decide to go ahead and answer them anyway. Others who decide to leave the demographic questions blank will probably return the mostly completed questionnaire, giving you answers to most of your questions. If the demographic questions had been at the beginning of the questionnaire, these individuals might not have answered any of your questions.

Guideline 3.8   Group together demographic questions and write a brief, separate introduction to them.

Your questionnaire should have an overall introduction, which we will consider in Chapter 7. In addition, it's a good idea to include a brief, separate introduction to the demographic questions. This introduction can be as casual and brief as the introduction shown in Example 3.8.1. Notice that it tells respondents why the information is needed and reassures them that the information will remain confidential.

Example 3.8.1

To put your answers in context, we'd like to gather some personal information from you. Of course, your answers will be held in the strictest confidence.

You might consider adding the heading "Optional Questions" just above the introduction to the demographic questions. This will let respondents know that you are interested in their answers to the other items even if they do not answer the demographic ones.

Exercise for Chapter 3

Directions: Answer the items in the spaces. *Note that there may be defensible differences of opinion on the answers to some of the items.*

1. Compare the following items (A and B) on religious affiliation. In your opinion, is one superior to the other? Would you make any changes in either of the items? Explain.

   Item A for Question 1:

   What is your religious affiliation?
   ☐ Atheist
   ☐ Agnostic
   ☐ Buddhist
   ☐ Catholic
   ☐ Hindu
   ☐ Jewish
   ☐ Muslim
   ☐ Protestant
   ☐ Other: _____

   Item B for Question 1:

   What is your religious affiliation?
   ☐ Protestant
   ☐ Catholic
   ☐ Jewish
   ☐ Muslim
   ☐ Other. Please specify: _____

2. Compare the following items (C and D) on race/ethnicity. In your opinion, is one superior to the other? Would you make any changes in either of the items? Explain.

   Item C for Question 2:

   What is your race?
   ☐ Asian
   ☐ Black
   ☐ Hispanic
   ☐ White
   ☐ Other

Item D for Question 2:

What is your race/ethnic group?
☐ African American
☐ Caucasian
☐ Asian American
☐ Pacific Islander
☐ Hispanic/Latino
☐ Other: _____

3. Compare the following items (E, F, G and H) on age. In your opinion, is one superior to the others? Would you make any changes in any of the items? Explain.

Item E for Question 3:

Your age: ☐

Item F for Question 3:

Your age (day/month/year): _____

Item G for Question 3:

Age?
☐ Under 18
☐ 18–25
☐ 26–35
☐ 36–50
☐ 51–75
☐ Over 75

Item H for Question 3:

Your age? ☐ Under 20 ☐ 20–24 ☐ 25–29 ☐ 30–34 ☐ 35–39 ☐ 40–44
☐ 45–49   ☐ 50–54 ☐ 55–59 ☐ 60–64 ☐ 65 and over

4. In your opinion, are there any flaws in the item shown immediately below?

Item for Question 4:

I am in a relationship.   _____Yes   _____No

5. In your opinion, are there any flaws in the item shown immediately below?

   Item for Question 5: (Note: This item appeared on a questionnaire for college students.)

   Your living arrangement. Please check one.
   ☐ On campus
   ☐ Off campus
   ☐ With parents

6. In your opinion, are there any flaws in the item shown immediately below?

   Item for Question 6:

   What is your level of education?
   ☐ High school degree or less
   ☐ Some college
   ☐ College degree
   ☐ Post-graduate degree or more

7. In your opinion, are there any flaws in the item shown immediately below?

   Item for Question 7:

   What is your GPA? _____

8. In your opinion, are there any flaws in the item shown immediately below?

   Item for Question 8:

   In what region of the country do you live?
   A. North
   B. South
   C. East
   D. West

9. In your opinion, are there any flaws in the item shown immediately below?

   Item for Question 9: (Note: This item was written for children.)

   What language do your parents usually speak at home? _____

10. In your opinion, are there any flaws in the item shown immediately below?

Item for Question 10:

Do you live alone?
☐ Yes   ☐ No ⤵

   If no, with whom do you live?
      ☐ family member
      ☐ nonfamily member

11. Consider the objectives that you wrote for item 8 in the Exercise for Chapter 1. Name one demographic variable that you might measure if you conducted research to achieve the objectives. Write an item to measure the variable.

Chapter 4

Writing Items to Measure Attitudes

In Chapters 2 and 3, we considered how to collect factual and demographic information using questionnaires. In this chapter, we will consider how questionnaires can be used to measure attitudes. An *attitude* is a general predisposition toward groups of people, organizations, institutions, and so on. When we measure attitudes, we ask questions about *feelings*, *actions*, and *potential actions*. Consider, for example, *attitude toward school*. To measure this, we could write items that ask respondents how they *feel* about doing their homework assignments, about participating in classroom discussions, about their interactions with their teachers, and so on. We could also ask about how they *act* with questions about playing hooky, trying their best when working on class projects, and so on. In addition, we could ask about *potential actions* such as whether they would drop out of school if allowed to do so.

Typically, we measure an attitude with a number of items. For instance, to get an adequate sample of the various feelings, actions, and potential actions that make up students' attitudes toward school, we might need 20 or more items. Such a collection of items is called an *attitude scale*, which can be used to get one overall attitude score for each respondent. In contrast, when we write a very small number of items about a specific element of schooling, such as the adequacy of a textbook, we tend to say that we are measuring *opinions*. While most of this chapter deals with how to construct attitude scales, we will come back to the measurement of opinions at the end of this chapter and in the next chapter.

Guideline 4.1   Examine attitude scales that have already been developed.

Researchers have written thousands of attitude scales. A good way to locate them is to consult the ERIC Clearinghouse on Assessment and Evaluation on the Internet at "http://www.ericae.net" (type everything within the quotation marks, but do *not* type the quotation marks).[1] You can find attitude scales by clicking on "Test Locator" and then scrolling down to "ETS Test File." Conduct a search by typing "attitudes toward computers" if you want to locate scales that measure attitudes toward computers. The Test File describes over 10,000 tests and scales,

---

[1] If you do not have access to the Internet, you should either contact the reference librarian at a college or university library, or write to Educational Testing Service, Princeton, NJ 08541.

many of which measure attitudes. There you will find descriptions of scales that measure attitudes as diverse as attitude toward the homeless, attitude toward rape, attitude toward math, and attitude toward female professors. In addition to describing available scales, the Test File indicates how to obtain copies of them.

When selecting a previously developed attitude scale, keep in mind that they vary in quality, and you will need to consider their merits carefully. Even if none meets your standards or is on-target for your research, you will probably get useful ideas on how to word and format attitude questions by examining attitude scales annotated in the Test File.

Guideline 4.2   Consider using Likert-type items.

In the 1930s, Rensis Likert advocated the use of items that ask respondents to indicate the extent to which they agree or disagree with statements.

To write a Likert-type item, write a simple declarative statement such as the one shown in Example 4.2.1 and follow it with choices that ask for the respondents' level of agreement.

Example 4.2.1

Physicians should be allowed to prescribe marijuana to relieve terminally ill cancer patients' symptoms.
☐ Strongly agree   ☐ Agree   ☐ Neutral   ☐ Disagree   ☐ Strongly disagree

Some item writers contend that "Agree" and "Disagree" are strong, absolute terms and have suggested substitutes. For example, instead of using "Agree" as a choice, they suggest using "Tend to agree," or "Agree somewhat." Respondents, on the other hand, do not seem to mind "Agree" and "Disagree" as choices, and research has failed to show that one set of choices is superior to the other.

Likert-type items can have up to about seven choices without requiring respondents to make falsely fine distinctions. A set of seven choices is: "Very strongly agree," "Strongly agree," "Agree," "Neutral," "Disagree," "Strongly disagree," and "Very strongly disagree." However, for most research purposes, the five choices shown in Example 4.2.1 are adequate.[2]

Since 1930, other item types have been developed to measure attitudes. Interestingly, extensive research indicates that none are clearly superior to Likert-type items, which are easy to write and easy for respondents to understand.

---

[2] The use of "Neutral" or "Undecided" as a middle choice is discussed in Guideline 4.4.

Guideline 4.3   The statement in a Likert-type item should deal with only one point.

Be careful not to inadvertently ask about two separate points in a single item, which was done in Example 4.3.1. The improved version allows respondents to indicate different responses for the two situations.

Example 4.3.1

I would approve of interethnic dating by my relatives and friends.
☐ Strongly agree   ☐ Agree   ☐ Disagree   ☐ Strongly disagree

Improved Version of Example 4.3.1

1. I would approve of interethnic dating by my relatives.
   ☐ Strongly agree   ☐ Agree   ☐ Disagree   ☐ Strongly disagree

2. I would approve of interethnic dating by my friends.
   ☐ Strongly agree   ☐ Agree   ☐ Disagree   ☐ Strongly disagree

Guideline 4.4   Consider whether to use "Neutral" or "Undecided" in Likert-type items.

The presence of "Neutral" or "Undecided" may encourage some respondents to take the lazy way out rather than ponder an item. This choice may also be attractive to respondents who do not wish to reveal their position on a controversial topic. On the other hand, the absence of a middle position may be frustrating to respondents who truly are neutral. Thus, whether to include this middle choice is a judgment call. If you believe that all your potential respondents probably have developed positive or negative attitudes toward the object of your scale, you may wish to omit "Neutral" or "Undecided." When it is omitted, you may want to include general directions that instruct respondents to select the choice in each item that is *closest* to their position. This may help to relieve the frustration of those who are basically neutral but are leaning very slightly one way or the other.

Note that when "Neutral" or "Undecided" is used as a choice, it should be listed as the middle choice. Also, note that these choices are *not* equivalent to "Don't know," which is discussed in the next guideline.

Guideline 4.5   Use "Don't know" sparingly in Likert-type items.

It is appropriate to include "Don't know" as a choice if you believe that some of your respondents may have very little or no knowledge of the object of the attitude you are measuring. For example, during the war in Bosnia, polls showed that many individuals in the United States had very little knowledge of the war. Thus, it would be appropriate to include "Don't know" in the items in an attitude scale designed to measure attitudes toward U.S. involvement in foreign conflicts when people may be unfamiliar with the specifics of the conflicts. The inclusion of "Don't know" as a choice is illustrated in Example 4.5.1.[3]

Example 4.5.1

Directions: For each statement, indicate your level of agreement by checking a box. If you do not have enough information about a statement to determine your level of agreement, leave the boxes blank and put an X in the box next to "Don't know."

1. The United States should give more military support to the Muslims in Bosnia.
   ☐ Strongly agree   ☐ Agree   ☐ Neutral   ☐ Disagree   ☐ Strongly disagree
   ☐ Don't know

Notice that "Don't know" should be set off from the other choices as in Example 4.5.1, where it is given on a separate line.[4] It should *not* be used as a middle choice (even if "Neutral" has been omitted as a choice) because "Don't know" is *not* a level of agreement; that is, it does *not* indicate a level of agreement that falls somewhere between "Agree" and "Disagree." Note that if "Don't know" is placed in the middle, some respondents may mistake it as meaning neutral or undecided. Of course, not knowing about a topic is not the same as being neutral toward it.

When incorporating "Don't know" as a choice in items, it is desirable to provide directions on how to use this choice, as was done in Example 4.5.1.

Guideline 4.6   Use multiple items in an attitude scale.

This guideline was alluded to in the introduction to this chapter, but it deserves additional comment.

Most attitudes, such as attitude toward work, are complex constructs consisting of many elements. A respondent may have positive feelings toward

---

[3] Some item writers use "no basis for judgment," "not applicable," or "not observed" instead of "don't know."

[4] You may also set it off by putting it at the beginning or the end of the line that contains the other choices.

some elements and negative ones toward others. Asking only a global question, such as the one in Example 4.6.1 to measure attitude toward work, oversimplifies the construct.

Example 4.6.1

I am satisfied with my job.
☐ Strongly agree   ☐ Agree   ☐ Disagree   ☐ Strongly disagree

A better measure of attitude toward work can be obtained by writing a series of items about the desire to be employed, the need to be productive, the willingness to follow directions on the job, internal and external rewards of working, and so on. Thus, it may be necessary to write a number of items to get a comprehensive measure of attitudes toward such a complex construct. Note that, as it stands, the item in Example 4.6.1 measures a general *opinion* about the respondent's specific job—not the broad construct of attitude toward work.

How many items you should write depends, in part, on the number of salient traits or characteristics people associate with the construct. Salient characteristics are those that stand out in respondents' minds; the ones listed in the previous paragraph are likely to be salient. In contrast, the color of the walls in workplaces is an example of a characteristic that probably is not very salient for most respondents. You can determine what is salient by examining literature on the topic. If there is little literature or if you believe that it may be misleading, you can determine salient characteristics by conducting a preliminary study with 10 to 15 respondents using open-ended questions such as, "What is the first thing that comes to your mind when you think about work?" and "What four things about your work and workplace are most important to you?" Common answers to these questions will give you suitable ideas for items.

If you identify a large number of salient characteristics, you may need to prune them to a reasonable number. Including more than about 25 items in an attitude scale may be perceived as a burden by some respondents, leading them to not respond. In Chapter 6, we will consider how to use a statistical technique called "item analysis" in order to select the best items from a large pool of potential items.

Guideline 4.7   Prepare a list of the broad components of an attitude, and use it as the basis for writing an attitude scale.

To see how this guideline works, suppose you were going to write a questionnaire to measure the attitudes of public school teachers toward the teaching profession. First, break the teaching profession into components such as:

(1) wages and benefits, (2) psychological rewards of teaching, (3) status of teaching in society, (4) interactions with children, (5) interactions with administrators, (6) interactions with parents, (7) interactions with other teachers, (8) physical/financial constraints on being an effective teacher, (9) educational requirements to enter the teaching profession, (10) opportunities for advancement, and so on.

You can use the components that you listed as the basis for a pilot study designed to determine the specific characteristics to ask about in an attitude scale. For example, you might ask a small number of teachers, "What are the first things that come to your mind when you think about the wages and benefits you earn as a teacher?" and "How important are wages and benefits to you?" The first question will yield information on the specific characteristics of wages and benefits on which you might write items. The second question will give you information on how important each characteristic is to the respondents. Those components that are judged to be more important usually should be given more emphasis in an attitude scale.

This process assures the construction of an adequately thought-out attitude scale — each item relates to a component, and the specific content of each item is based on the responses of a small sample of respondents.

Guideline 4.8   In an attitude scale, make some statements favorable and others unfavorable.

Let's suppose you've written a number of items designed to measure attitude toward math, and all of them make favorable statements about math. Part of such a series is shown in Example 4.8.1. Some respondents may respond to all items in the series in a global fashion. For example, someone with a very positive attitude toward math might simply mark them all "Strongly agree" without carefully considering each item. Responding in this way (based on a general impression or attitude) is known as the *halo effect*. In addition, those who write attitude scales need to be concerned with *response sets*. For example, some individuals have an "acquiescence" response set in that they tend to agree with everything. Others may tend to be negative regardless of the topic. Still others may tend to respond to everything with a neutral position to avoid taking a stand. Writing some items so that they are favorable and others so they are unfavorable, which was done in the improved version, is believed to help break down these response sets and reduce the influence of the halo effect. At the very least, this technique will slow down respondents, which may lead to more careful consideration of the content of individual items.

Example 4.8.1 *Four of the 25 items in an attitude-toward-math scale:*

1. I like doing my math homework.
   ☐ Strongly agree   ☐ Agree   ☐ Disagree   ☐ Strongly disagree

2. Math is one of my favorite subjects in school.
   ☐ Strongly agree   ☐ Agree   ☐ Disagree   ☐ Strongly disagree

3. I would rather solve math problems than write an essay.
   ☐ Strongly agree   ☐ Agree   ☐ Disagree   ☐ Strongly disagree

4. I enjoy reading my math textbook.
   ☐ Strongly agree   ☐ Agree   ☐ Disagree   ☐ Strongly disagree

Improved Version of Example 4.8.1

1. I like doing my math homework.
   ☐ Strongly agree   ☐ Agree   ☐ Disagree   ☐ Strongly disagree

2. Math is one of my least favorite subjects in school.
   ☐ Strongly agree   ☐ Agree   ☐ Disagree   ☐ Strongly disagree

3. I would rather solve math problems than write an essay.
   ☐ Strongly agree   ☐ Agree   ☐ Disagree   ☐ Strongly disagree

4. I dislike reading my math textbook.
   ☐ Strongly agree   ☐ Agree   ☐ Disagree   ☐ Strongly disagree

Avoid using "not" to create the statements that are unfavorable because research has shown that "not" in an item can cause confusion. Thus, in the Improved Version of Example 4.8.1, the second statement is "Math is one of my least favorite subjects in school" *instead of* "Math is not one of my favorite subjects in school."

Of course, you need to be careful when scoring and interpreting items such as those in the Improved Version of Example 4.8.1. Marking "Strongly agree" to the first item needs to be scored in the opposite direction than marking "Strongly agree" to the second item. Scoring attitude scales is discussed under Guideline 6.7 in Chapter 6.

Guideline 4.9   Consider asking about reactions to hypothetical situations when necessary.

Notice that in Example 4.8.1 above, the items ask about feelings in reaction to experiences that almost everyone has had (for example, feelings about reading a math textbook). Sometimes, however, it is necessary to ask about hypothetical experiences. For example, suppose you wanted to measure attitudes toward people who are HIV+. If it is likely that many of your respondents do not personally know anyone who is HIV+, you may wish to establish a hypothetical situation and ask respondents how they would feel and act in response. Example 4.9.1 illustrates this technique.

Example 4.9.1[5]

Directions: Suppose a new classmate told you that he or she is HIV+. Answer the following questions about your reactions.

1. I would avoid spending time with the person.
   □ Strongly agree   □ Agree   □ Disagree   □ Strongly disagree

2. I would treat the person just as I would anyone else.
   □ Strongly agree   □ Agree   □ Disagree   □ Strongly disagree

3. I would stay away from club meetings if that person joined the club.
   □ Strongly agree   □ Agree   □ Disagree   □ Strongly disagree

4. I would consider becoming friends with the person.
   □ Strongly agree   □ Agree   □ Disagree   □ Strongly disagree

5. I would ask to be transferred to another class.
   □ Strongly agree   □ Agree   □ Disagree   □ Strongly disagree

6. I would find it difficult to concentrate on my schoolwork with the person in the classroom.
   □ Strongly agree   □ Agree   □ Disagree   □ Strongly disagree

7. I would welcome the person to the class.
   □ Strongly agree   □ Agree   □ Disagree   □ Strongly disagree

8. I would be afraid of getting HIV.
   □ Strongly agree   □ Agree   □ Disagree   □ Strongly disagree

9. I would feel comfortable playing on a sports team with the person.
   □ Strongly agree   □ Agree   □ Disagree   □ Strongly disagree

Notice that the item writer has asked about attitudes in one specific hypothetical situation (that is, having a new classmate who is HIV+). This will

---

[5] The term "HIV+" should be defined in the directions unless the item writer believes that all respondents are familiar with the term. For example, if the attitude scale is being administered to students who just completed a comprehensive unit on HIV/AIDS, it may not be necessary to define it.

limit the generalizability of the findings obtained with this scale because it does not tap attitudes in other situations.

Also, note that while responses to hypothetical situations provide interesting information that, on the whole, reflect general attitudes, there is extensive anecdotal evidence and some research showing that how people say they would react to a hypothetical situation sometimes fails to match their actual reactions when confronted with the real situation. Thus, attitude measurements based on hypothetical situations should be interpreted as indicating a current predisposition — not as indicating how the attitude would manifest itself under actual circumstances.

Guideline 4.10   Only use items that are clearly indicative of a favorable or unfavorable attitude.

Failure to follow this guideline is often inadvertent. For example, when an item writer wrote the items in Example 4.10.1, she thought that a response of "Strongly agree" or "Agree" would indicate a negative attitude toward people who are HIV+. Later, she realized that "being concerned" and "reacting strongly" could be taken both ways. For example, in response to the first item, one respondent may be very concerned in a positive way about the health and welfare of the new classmate, while another may be very concerned because he or she is fearful of contracting HIV. Thus, the item is ambiguous in terms of whether the item is indicative of a favorable or unfavorable attitude. The second item is also ambiguous because a strong reaction could be in either the positive or negative direction. Such items can often be identified when you try out the items and perform an item analysis. We will consider these topics in Chapter 6.

Example 4.10.1

Directions: Suppose a new classmate told you that he or she was HIV+. Answer the following questions about your reactions to this information.

1. I would feel very concerned.
   ☐ Strongly agree   ☐ Agree   ☐ Disagree   ☐ Strongly disagree

2. I would react strongly to his or her presence in the classroom.
   ☐ Strongly agree   ☐ Agree   ☐ Disagree   ☐ Strongly disagree

Guideline 4.11   Label each point in a Likert-type item.

It was pointed out earlier that respondents can handle up to about seven choices in a Likert-type item without being forced to make falsely fine distinctions. Each point on the scale should be labeled with words. Do *not* write items such as the one in Example 4.11.1, which contains too many choices that are not labeled individually. Such an item leaves respondents wondering, for example, what the difference is between an 8 and a 7.

Example 4.11.1

Thinking about using a computer makes me anxious. (Circle one number.)
Strongly agree   10 9 8 7 6 5 4 3 2 1 0   Strongly disagree

Guideline 4.12   Consider using a double-column format to present Likert-type items.

An efficient format for presenting Likert-type items is to list the statements in the first column and the choices in the columns to the right, as illustrated in Example 4.12.1.

Example 4.12.1

The following statements refer to **Asian Americans**. Please indicate your level of agreement with each statement by placing a check mark in the appropriate box.

	Strongly agree	Agree	Neutral	Disagree	Strongly disagree
1. I would welcome them as next-door neighbors.	☐	☐	☐	☐	☐
2. They make a positive contribution to the nation's economy.	☐	☐	☐	☐	☐
3. They should stay in their own neighborhoods.	☐	☐	☐	☐	☐
4. They put a strain on the welfare system.	☐	☐	☐	☐	☐

Guideline 4.13   Use simplified choices for children.

Up to about grade 2, questionnaires should be read aloud to groups of children. For young children, happy, neutral, and sad faces have been used effectively as choices. The test administrator reads statements such as "Circle the face that shows how you feel when you do your math homework." When using this technique, it is a good idea to put each item on separate, color-coded pages. Color-coding can be as simple as having green pages alternate with white pages. With coding, the researcher can glance around the room to make sure that all children are responding on the correct page for each item. Example 4.13.1 shows what might appear on a page that children mark. Note that the words are provided for children who are able to read them, even though the teacher will be reading the items aloud. Also, note that you should use a larger font for young children than you would use for older children and adults.

Example 4.13.1[6]

(*Note*: Teacher says, "Circle the face that shows how you feel when you do your math homework.")

How you feel when you do your math homework.

For slightly older children, "Yes" and "No" or "True" and "False" may be used instead of the usual "Strongly agree" to "Strongly disagree" choices. This is illustrated in Examples 4.13.2 and 4.13.3.

Example 4.13.2

Circle "yes" or "no" for each question.

1. Do you like doing your math homework?

   Yes   No

2. Is math boring?

   Yes   No

Example 4.13.3

Circle true or false for each sentence.

1. I enjoy doing my math homework.

   True   False

2. Math is boring.

   True   False

The yes-no format is usually better than the true-false format because the latter is associated with tests on which there are right and wrong answers. In an attitude scale, of course, the only "right" answers are those that indicate the

---

[6] Using a modern word processing program, you can produce the faces by copying them from the character map for the Wingdings font.

respondents' true feelings. If the true-false format is used, the directions should indicate that there are no right or wrong answers.

When in doubt about children's ability to read the words in items such as those in Examples 4.13.2 and 4.13.3, read the items aloud to the children.

Concluding Comment

Attitude scales typically contain 20 or more items, all relating to the same construct. So that your respondents can move easily through the items without having to keep changing gears, it is recommended that all your items contain simple statements followed by "Strongly agree" to "Strongly disagree" choices. For young children, simplified choices can be used. In the next chapter, we will explore how to measure *opinions* in order to evaluate products, services, and programs. There you will find more variety in item formats.

Exercise for Chapter 4

Directions: Answer the items in the spaces. *Note that there may be defensible differences of opinion on the answers to some of the items.*

1. What is the name for the type of item that asks respondents to indicate their level of agreement with a simple statement? (Hint: It is named for the man who first suggested it.)

2. Describe the flaw(s) in the following item.

   I believe in God and feel close to him.
   ☐ Strongly agree   ☐ Agree   ☐ Neutral   ☐ Disagree   ☐ Strongly disagree

3. Name one argument for *not* including "Neutral" or "Undecided" as a choice.

4. Name one argument for including "Neutral" or "Undecided" as a choice.

5. If you include "Don't know" as a choice, should it be placed in the middle of the other choices in a Likert-type item? Why? Why not?

6. In your opinion, is it appropriate to include "Don't know" in the following item? Explain.

   The school district should permit more schools to join the ListTech Program.
   ☐ Strongly agree   ☐ Agree   ☐ Undecided   ☐ Disagree   ☐ Strongly disagree
   ☐ Don't know

7. Under most circumstances, would using the following item as the only item to measure attitudes toward physicians be adequate? Explain.

   Medical doctors do more harm than good.
   ☐ Strongly agree   ☐ Agree   ☐ Neutral   ☐ Disagree   ☐ Strongly disagree

8. What is meant by the term *salient characteristics*? Name three characteristics of computers and their uses that you consider sufficiently salient to use as the basis for items in a scale to measure employees' attitude toward computers.

9. Why should some Likert-type items in an attitude scale be favorable while others should be unfavorable?

10. Describe the flaw(s), if any, in the following item from a scale on attitude toward the legislative branch of the United States government.

    United States senators are powerful.
    ☐ Strongly agree   ☐ Agree   ☐ Neutral   ☐ Disagree   ☐ Strongly disagree

11. What are the simplified alternatives to using a "Strongly agree" to "Strongly disagree" set of choices for use with children?

12. If the research objectives you wrote for item 8 in the Exercise for Chapter 1 call for the measurement of attitudes, write four items designed to measure the attitude you specified.

Notes:

Chapter 5

Writing Items to Evaluate Products, Services, and Programs

We often use questionnaires to evaluate products, services, and programs. For example, questionnaires can measure students' evaluation of instruction (a service), consumers' satisfaction with automobiles, and welfare recipients' opinions on the food stamp program. In this chapter, we will consider how to write items for the purposes of evaluation.

Guideline 5.1 Name specific characteristics to be evaluated.

Since the major function of evaluation is to gather information that may be used to improve products, services, and programs, most items should deal with specific, unambiguous characteristics. Consider Example 5.1.1, which shows four items from a questionnaire. Notice that the traits to be evaluated are broad hypothetical constructs, which are inherently ambiguous. What if a professor gets low ratings on flexibility? Should she become more flexible on the requirement that students do homework? Should she become more flexible on the starting time of the class—starting it at different times each week? These types of problems in interpretation can be avoided by asking about specific characteristics, as shown in the Improved Version of Example 5.1.1.

Example 5.1.1 (Part of a student evaluation questionnaire.)

Please evaluate your professor in each of the following areas.
(Mark one box across for each item.)

	Excellent	Very good	Fair	Poor	Very poor
1. Flexible	☐	☐	☐	☐	☐
2. Fair	☐	☐	☐	☐	☐
3. Concerned	☐	☐	☐	☐	☐
4. Energetic	☐	☐	☐	☐	☐

Improved Version of Example 5.1.1 (Part of a student evaluation questionnaire.)

Please evaluate your professor in each of the following areas.
(Mark one box across for each item.)

	Excellent	Very good	Fair	Poor	Very poor
1. Is available to help outside of class.	☐	☐	☐	☐	☐
2. Encourages student participation in class.	☐	☐	☐	☐	☐
3. Uses appropriate tests and measures.	☐	☐	☐	☐	☐
4. Assigns appropriate reading material, including textbooks.	☐	☐	☐	☐	☐

Example 5.1.2 shows some items from a questionnaire for evaluating an automobile. Notice that the items are specific, which will allow the manufacturer to identify areas that need improvement *from the drivers' point of view*. Of course, the automobile manufacturer has already taken physical measures of all five items (for example, measured the automobile's interior space). The purpose of asking about them in a questionnaire is to determine the automobile owners' satisfaction with them.

Example 5.1.2

Please indicate your evaluation of your automobile in each of the following areas.

	Very satisfied	Moderately satisfied	Somewhat satisfied	Somewhat dissatisfied	Moderately dissatisfied	Very dissatisfied
1. Interior roominess	☐	☐	☐	☐	☐	☐
2. Ease of handling	☐	☐	☐	☐	☐	☐
3. Quietness	☐	☐	☐	☐	☐	☐
4. Operation of brakes	☐	☐	☐	☐	☐	☐
5. Power and pickup	☐	☐	☐	☐	☐	☐

Guideline 5.2   Consider including an item to solicit an overall evaluation.

It's a good idea to include an item asking for an overall evaluation—even though it does not refer to specific characteristics to be evaluated (see Guideline 5.1). For example, "Overall teaching ability" might be included as an item in a student evaluation questionnaire. Such a question will provide additional information since different students may emphasize different elements in arriving at their overall evaluation. For instance, one student might give low ratings on only a couple of items but feel that these items touch on very important characteristics of a professor, resulting in a low overall evaluation. Another student might also give low ratings on a couple of items but feel that these items deal with relatively unimportant characteristics, resulting in a high overall evaluation. Thus, an item requesting an overall evaluation provides a picture of the *whole*, while the other items on specific characteristics provide information on the specific *parts*.

Note that some researchers prefer to put an item asking for an overall evaluation first in a questionnaire while others prefer to put it last. Whether to put it first or last depends on what you wish to determine. If you want to determine respondents' overall evaluation only after they have considered specific characteristics referred to in earlier items, put it last. (Note that when an item asking for an overall evaluation is put last, respondents will tend to consider their earlier answers in arriving at their overall evaluation.) If you want to determine their overall evaluation without the possible influence of other items on a questionnaire, put it first.

Guideline 5.3   Consider including "Don't know" as a choice.

If some of your respondents have not had an opportunity to observe an element to be rated, provide "Don't know" as a choice. For example, the first item in the Improved Version of Example 5.1.1 asks about the availability of the professor to provide assistance outside of class. A student who has not sought such assistance is not in a position to evaluate this characteristic. Thus, the item could be improved further by adding "Don't know" as a choice.[1] On the other hand, an individual who owns a particular brand of automobile should have had the opportunity to evaluate all the characteristics in Example 5.1.2; thus, "Don't know" is not needed.

Guideline 5.4   Ask respondents to evaluate only salient characteristics.

Note that most products, services, and programs have a very large number of characteristics that might be evaluated. Since you will want your questionnaire to be efficient, ask only about salient characteristics. These are characteristics that stand out in respondents' minds because of their importance to them. You can determine which characteristics are salient by examining the literature on your topic or by conducting a preliminary study by asking 10 to 15 individuals general questions about the product, service, or program. For example, when preparing a

---

[1] Instead of "Don't know," you might consider using "No opportunity to observe," "No basis for judgment," or "Not applicable."

questionnaire to evaluate automobiles, you might ask a small number of individuals questions such as, "When you shop for a car, what things do you look for?," "What are the things you like most about your car?," and "What are the things you like least about your car?"

Guideline 5.5   Consider asking respondents if they would recommend the product, service, or program to others.

One of the most powerful influences in the marketplace for services, products, and programs is word of mouth. Thus, an item relating to this matter is often included in questionnaires designed for evaluation. Example 5.5.1 shows an example of such a question.

Example 5.5.1

Based on your experiences, would you recommend United Parcel Service to others?
☐ Definitely would
☐ Probably would
☐ Maybe would/Maybe not
☐ Probably would not
☐ Definitely would not

Guideline 5.6   When determining the content for items in a program evaluation, refer to the services and objectives stated in the proposal for the program.

The proposals for formal programs indicate what services will be provided (for example, group tutoring on job-seeking skills for welfare recipients) and the objectives for the clients (for example, getting a job in the private sector). Since programs are funded on the basis of their proposals, it is obvious that programs should be evaluated in terms of the services and objectives specified in their proposals. Questionnaires often can be used to help evaluate both aspects of a program.

Evaluating the process of delivering services is called *formative evaluation*.[2] For this type of evaluation, we can ask questions to determine from the client's point of view the extent to which the services were provided and their

---

[2] *Formative evaluation* also involves evaluating the extent to which clients are making *progress* toward the ultimate goals of a program.

degree of satisfaction with the services. Example 5.6.1 shows a set of items designed to elicit from patients whether certain services were provided in a health care program.

Example 5.6.1

Directions: Think about the <u>last time</u> you visited the clinic. Answer the questions based on that experience.

1. When you called the clinic for an appointment, was the phone answered promptly?   ☐ Yes   ☐ No

2. When you arrived for your last appointment, did the receptionist greet you by name?   ☐ Yes   ☐ No

3. Were you taken to an examination room within 15 minutes of arriving for your appointment?   ☐ Yes   ☐ No

While Example 5.6.1 shows items that ask about whether services were provided, Example 5.6.2 asks about patients' satisfaction with a service. Both types of items are appropriate in a formative evaluation.

Example 5.6.2

Directions: Think about the <u>last time</u> you visited the clinic. Indicate how satisfied you were with each of the following.

1. The willingness of the doctor to listen to you.
   ☐ Very satisfied
   ☐ Moderately satisfied
   ☐ Somewhat satisfied
   ☐ Somewhat dissatisfied
   ☐ Moderately dissatisfied
   ☐ Very dissatisfied

Note that a *formative evaluation* should be used to help guide (or form) the program. Thus, questionnaires for formative evaluation should be used periodically during the implementation of a program, and the results should be provided to the program's administrators and workers so that services can be improved as soon as possible.

Evaluating the outcomes of services is called *summative evaluation*. In our example, this calls for questions regarding the outcomes of medical treatment, such as "Was the diagnosis correct?," "Were the correct medications given?," and "Did the patient's condition improve?"

For a comprehensive evaluation, you will probably want to gather information in more than one way. For example, for a health care program, you might have the clinic's staff keep a log of the times when patients arrive and the times when they are taken to an examination room. For an educational program, you might need to give a test to see if students have acquired the skills and knowledge the program was designed to enhance.[3] You can determine their satisfaction with the program, however, by also administering a questionnaire to the clients of a program. Do they *believe* that they were taken promptly to the examination room? Do they *believe* that they learned a lot by participating in the educational program? Answers to questions such as these are valuable when considering the overall success of a program because they indicate the extent to which clients were satisfied with the services provided by the program and their perceptions of the extent to which they made progress or achieved goals as a result of the program.

Guideline 5.7   Consider asking some open-ended questions.

Providing a section labeled "Other comments" at the end of a questionnaire allows room for respondents to elaborate on their responses to earlier items and to address issues not covered by earlier items. Example 5.7.1 shows two items that make it clear that the evaluator is interested in both positive and negative comments.

Example 5.7.1

OTHER COMMENTS:

1. What, if anything, about your last visit to the clinic especially pleased you?

_____

_____

_____

2. What, if anything, about your last visit to the clinic especially disappointed you?

_____

_____

_____

You might also consider including open-ended questions that specifically ask respondents to explain any low ratings such as "Moderately dissatisfied" or "Very dissatisfied." Responses to them can help pinpoint the nature of the complaints. For example, one respondent may mark "dissatisfied" for "comfort of the driver's seat" in an automobile because its position makes it hard to get out of the car; another might mark the same choice because the seat is not firm enough;

---

[3] Many educational programs call for changing students' overall attitudes such as improving their attitude toward math. See Chapter 4 for a discussion of how attitudes can be measured with questionnaires.

another might mark it because it is difficult to adjust the position of the seat.[4] Explanations can help identify the specific source(s) of dissatisfaction.

Exercise for Chapter 5

1. The following items were designed as part of a questionnaire to evaluate a personal computer system, including peripherals such as a printer, scanner, and so on. Comment on the adequacy of the items.

	Very satisfied	Moderately satisfied	Somewhat satisfied	Somewhat dissatisfied	Moderately dissatisfied	Very dissatisfied
1. Speed	☐	☐	☐	☐	☐	☐
2. Size	☐	☐	☐	☐	☐	☐
3. Usefulness	☐	☐	☐	☐	☐	☐

2. When should you put an item on the overall evaluation at the end of a questionnaire? When should you put it at the beginning?

3. When should "Don't know" be included as a choice in an item?

4. How can you determine which characteristics of a product, service, or program are salient?

5. What should you refer to when determining which elements of a *program* to evaluate?

6. Briefly explain the difference between formative and summative evaluation.

---

[4] Of course, the evaluator could have used a separate question to ask about each possible source of dissatisfaction with the driver's seat. However, if this approach were taken with each major component of an automobile, the questionnaire probably would become too long for a typical survey. A component that consistently gets low ratings might be explored in more detail in a follow-up study.

7. The following items were used in a questionnaire to evaluate a workshop that teachers took on improving discipline in the classroom. Which item(s) relate to *formative* evaluation and which one(s) relate to *summative* evaluation?

	Excellent	Good	Fair	Poor	Very poor
1. Videos shown in the workshop.	☐	☐	☐	☐	☐
2. Length of the workshop.	☐	☐	☐	☐	☐
3. Ability of the presenters to hold my attention.	☐	☐	☐	☐	☐
4. Small group discussions in the workshop.	☐	☐	☐	☐	☐
5. My ability to handle discipline problems in my classroom as a result of the workshop.	☐	☐	☐	☐	☐

8. What are two reasons for asking some open-ended questions in a questionnaire designed for evaluation of a product, service, or program?

9. If the objectives you wrote for item 8 in the Exercise for Chapter 1 indicate that you will be evaluating a product, service, or program, write at least three items that you might use in a questionnaire for this purpose.

Chapter 6

Conducting Item Tryouts and an Item Analysis

By trying out your items before using them in your main study, you usually will be able to improve your questionnaire and, thus, the validity of your results. If limited time and resources prevent you from following all the guidelines in this chapter, at least follow the first three.

Note that the guidelines usually should be followed in the order presented below. After following each guideline, revise any problematic items before moving on to the next guideline.

Guideline 6.1   Have your items reviewed by others.

It is especially helpful to have people who are experienced in writing questionnaires review the first drafts of your questions. If you are using this book in a college-level class, it is also a very good idea to have your classmates review the items.

Items that cause discussion should be viewed with suspicion. If you find yourself having to explain the items to your reviewers, you probably need to revise them.

Try to avoid becoming defensive when discussing your items with reviewers. If they sense that you are becoming even slightly defensive, they may stop offering their criticisms in order to avoid offending or antagonizing you.

Guideline 6.2   Conduct "think-alouds" with several people.

Ask several individuals who will *not* be respondents in your main study to answer the items while thinking aloud. Explain that you want them to say aloud what they are thinking while they are considering the items. Of course, this should be done with one individual at a time. Consider using a tape recorder so you can review their thoughts carefully at a later time.

The main function of a think-aloud is to identify items that are ambiguous. For example, in response to the question in Example 6.2.1, a college student said, "Well, I went to the college library once, and I called the reference librarian at the city library once, so the answer is 2." If the item writer really wants to know how many times respondents physically entered the college library, the item should be modified in light of this student's response. A better item would be "How often did you go to the college library in the last week?"

Example 6.2.1

How often did you use the library in the last week? _____ (number of times)

Think-alouds can also reveal other types of problems. For instance, in response to the question in Example 6.2.2, a professor said, "I usually find a parking spot right away, but sometimes I have trouble finding one. It seems like every time I have a problem finding one, it's when I'm running late. I guess the answer is no." This response suggests that the "Yes—No" format is probably inappropriate since the professor *usually* finds it adequate but answers "No" because she sometimes has difficulty finding a parking space. Thus, it probably would be better to ask for the degree of satisfaction with the adequacy of parking on a scale from "Very satisfied" to "Very dissatisfied."

Example 6.2.2

Is campus parking adequate?   ☐ Yes   ☐ No

Conduct a think-aloud for a set of items, and you may well find that one or more items that seemed perfectly clear to you are in need of improvement.

Guideline 6.3   Carefully select individuals for think-alouds.

Suppose you have written questionnaire items about a new campus policy on date rape. Since men and women may differ on their opinions, you probably will want to use one or two men and one or two women for your think-alouds.[1] On the other hand, suppose you have written questions to use in an evaluation of a workshop for teachers on using computers in the classroom. For your think-alouds, you may want to identify one or two teachers who are very experienced, one or two who are moderately experienced, and one or two who are relatively inexperienced in using computers in the classroom because you may get different types of information from teachers with different levels of experience. For example, if you slip up and use a difficult, technical computer term, it may confuse inexperienced teachers and be identified as a problem in your think-alouds with them. If you had used only experienced teachers, the problem might not have been identified in the think-alouds.

---

[1] For participation in your think-alouds, note that you could use stratified random sampling to select individuals from the population of those who will not be in your main study. This method of sampling is discussed in Chapter 8.

Guideline 6.4   Consider asking about 10 individuals to write detailed responses on a draft of your questionnaire.

To the extent possible, format your questionnaire with wide margins and plenty of white space among items for this type of item tryout. Ask about 10 individuals who are similar to those you will be using in your main study to mark one choice per item *and* write comments in the margins about anything they find confusing, that needs more explanation, or that is in error. Even though many of the notes they write may be cryptic (most people avoid writing essays), you probably will get useful information from this step in questionnaire development.

Of course, you do *not* want the larger number of respondents in your main study to write comments in the margins. By collecting written comments from about 10 individuals while the questionnaire is still a draft, you may get information that is useful in reworking and improving items so that the respondents in your main study will not be tempted to write marginal notes to you.

Guideline 6.5   Ask 25 or more respondents to respond to the questionnaire for an item analysis.

In an item analysis, respondents who will not be taking part in the main study are asked to respond to the questionnaire so that the responses can be statistically analyzed as indicated under the next two guidelines. Ideally, the respondents for an item analysis should be drawn at random (such as drawing names from a hat).[2] If this is not possible, at least attempt to get respondents whose relevant characteristics match those who will take part in the main study. For example, you may need to use students at your university for the item analysis even though you will be mailing the questionnaire to university students throughout the country.

Guideline 6.6   In the first stage of an item analysis, tally the number of respondents who selected each choice.

It's usually helpful to convert the tallies into percentages. For example, if 4 out of 25 respondents mark "Excellent," the percentage is $4/25 = .16 \times 100 = 16\%$.

---

[2] Other methods of drawing random samples are discussed in Chapter 8.

Examine the tallies or percentages to identify choices marked by few or no respondents. Example 6.6.1 shows the percentages who marked the choices for an item designed for use with high school students. Notice that the last two choices are dead wood because no one selected them. In addition, most of the important information on how often cocaine is used is lost since almost everyone marked the first choice. Since this choice goes from zero to ten, it is not clear whether most of them have not used it (that is, zero times) or used it up to 10 times. Based on the item analysis, the item was revised, as shown in the Improved Version of Example 6.6.1. Included in this example are the percentages that were obtained in a second item analysis. Clearly, the improved version provides more information on the frequency of cocaine use.

Example 6.6.1

How many times have you used cocaine in the last month?
☐ 0 to 10 times   ☐ 11 to 20 times   ☐ 21 to 30 times   ☐ 31 times or more
    99%   1%   0%   0%

Improved Version of Example 6.6.1

How many times have you used cocaine in the last month?
☐ 0 times   ☐ 1 to 3 times   ☐ 4 to 6 times   ☐ 7 to 9 times   ☐ 10 times or more
   80%   14%   3%   2%   1%

Consider another example that illustrates this stage of item analysis. In a product evaluation questionnaire, a computer manufacturer asked consumers to rate various hardware components of a computer system. The percentages who marked each choice in their evaluation of the keyboard are shown in Example 6.6.2. Since almost everyone was very satisfied and no one was dissatisfied, the manufacturer might consider eliminating the item from the questionnaire to make it shorter or to use the space for an item on some other component in the computer system.

Example 6.6.2

	Very satisfied	Moderately satisfied	Somewhat satisfied	Somewhat dissatisfied	Moderately dissatisfied	Very dissatisfied
1. Keyboard	95%	5%	0%	0%	0%	0%

Note that an item should not be omitted automatically just because an item analysis revealed that the item failed to differentiate among respondents because all, or nearly all, of them selected the same choice. Consider, for example, an item on the overall effectiveness of a workshop for business managers on computer networking. Even if all respondents in an item analysis indicate that they are very satisfied, the item should probably remain in the questionnaire since the information that all were very satisfied will be important when evaluating the workshop. Conversely, if all indicated that they were very dissatisfied, this information will be crucial for the workshop leaders. Thus, an item should be eliminated at this stage of item analysis only if its omission will not cause the loss of needed information.

Guideline 6.7 In the second stage of an item analysis, compare the responses of high and low groups on individual items.

In order to conduct this stage of an item analysis, you must be able to identify respondents who are high and low on a single hypothetical construct. Of the various types of instruments considered in this book, generally only attitude scales meet this criterion. For example, consider a 25-item scale on attitudes toward statistics that was administered to students in an introductory statistics class shortly after the midterm examination. We can score each item for each respondent and sum the item scores to get a total score for the construct "attitude toward statistics." Example 6.7.1 shows how the total score for an individual on four of the items (two expressing positive feelings and two expressing negative feelings) could be obtained.

Example 6.7.1

Four of the 25 items with the choices marked by one respondent:

1. I enjoy doing my statistics homework. ☐ SA ☐ A ☐ N ☐ D ☑ SD

2. Statistics is confusing. ☐ SA ☑ A ☐ N ☐ D ☐ SD

3. Taking statistics is a waste of my time. ☐ SA ☑ A ☐ N ☐ D ☐ SD

4. Statistics has many useful applications in
   everyday life. ☐ SA ☐ A ☐ N ☑ D ☐ SD

Score points for items expressing positive feelings (items 1 and 4):
SA = 4, A = 3, N = 2, D = 1, SD = 0

Score points for items expressing negative feelings (items 2 and 3):
SA = 0, A = 1, N = 2, D = 3, SD = 4

Points awarded and total score on the four items:
1. Item 1 = 0 points
2. Item 2 = 1 point
3. Item 3 = 1 point
4. Item 4 = 1 point
   TOTAL = 3 points

Since there are 4 items in Example 6.7.1 with each item worth 0 to 4 points, the total scores could range from 0 to 16. We looked at only 4 items as an example to illustrate how to score attitude items to arrive at a total score. The complete attitude toward statistics scale had 25 items, so the possible score range is from 0 to 100 (i.e., 4 x 25 items = 100) for the full scale.

There are several ways to complete this stage of the item analysis.[3] We will consider the easiest one here. First, get a total score on the attitude scale for each respondent in the item analysis tryout. (Remember that about 25 is the minimum number of respondents, but more is better. For the examples we are about to examine, there were 36 respondents.) Second, select the 1/3 of the respondents who had the highest total scores (that is, the top scoring 1/3, which is 12 of the 36 respondents) and the bottom scoring 1/3. Then, tally their responses to individual items separately as shown in Example 6.7.2.

Example 6.7.2

Item: I enjoy doing my statistics homework.

Response	SA	A	N	D	SD
Tallies for the 12 with the highest total scores:	///	/////	//	/	/
Tallies for the 12 with the lowest total scores:		/	///	////	////

Notice that those who have the highest total scores (indicating that they are favorably disposed toward statistics) tend to agree with the statement in Example 6.7.2, while those with the lowest total scores tend to disagree. This indicates that the item in Example 6.7.2 is discriminating properly; that is, this item is providing proper discrimination between the highest and lowest scorers. From the point of view of this stage of item analysis, this item is working correctly.

The value of looking at an item's ability to discriminate is clearer when we have an item that is not discriminating properly, as illustrated in Example 6.7.3. Notice that the pattern of response for the top scoring respondents is similar to the pattern for the lowest; that is, those with the most favorable attitudes toward statistics had a similar response pattern to the item as those who had the least favorable attitudes. Thus, the validity of the item is called into question. When facing data such as these, the item writer should reconsider the item. Is the item clear and unambiguous? Is it really measuring some facet of attitudes toward statistics? Upon consideration, the answer to the second question seems to be "No." The perception that statistics has many details seems to be common among

---

[3] If you feel comfortable with statistics, you may wish to correlate the scores on each item with the total test scores. Items that have a correlation of .30 or less with the total scores may be unclear, ambiguous, or contain other flaws. Correlation coefficients are discussed in Chapter 11.

those with positive attitudes and those with negative attitudes. Thus, this item does not contribute to the overall measure of attitude toward statistics.

Example 6.7.3

Item: There are many details in statistics.

Response	SA	A	N	D	SD
Tallies for the 12 with the highest total scores:	/////	////	//	/	
Tallies for the 12 with the lowest total scores:	///// //	////	/		

Many different types of patterns may emerge when conducting this phase of item analysis. However, there are two general principles to follow when considering them. First, do the differences make sense in light of the fact that the two groups have very different overall attitudes toward statistics as indicated by total scores on all the items? If not, the item needs to be reconsidered. Second, do not over-interpret small differences. For example, if one respondent in the bottom scoring group marks "Strongly agree" in response to "I enjoy doing my statistics homework," don't automatically suspect that the item is flawed. Remember that some respondents may be careless or simply be unique in their reactions.

Concluding Comment

Conducting item tryouts and the first stage of item analysis are essential if you want the items in your questionnaire to be of the highest quality. The second stage of item analysis is very important for identifying flawed items in attitude scales. Professional researchers know the value of the guidelines in this chapter and follow them routinely when developing questionnaires.

Exercise for Chapter 6

1. What directions should you give someone who will be participating in a think-aloud for you?

2. Suppose you were going to conduct think-alouds to refine a questionnaire on attitudes toward the automobile insurance industry. What type(s) of individuals would you select? (See Guideline 6.3).

3. About how many individuals should be asked to write marginal notes on a questionnaire?

4. About how many individuals should be asked to take a questionnaire for item-analysis purposes?

5. What should you calculate in the first stage of item analysis?

6. What should you consider doing if almost all respondents in an item analysis select the same choice in an item? Should you always do it? Explain.

7. Get a total score for an individual who marked the items below as indicated by check marks. (The items are just a sample of the 30 items in a scale designed to measure attitudes toward the jury system.) Use the score point system described under Guideline 6.7.

    1. The jury system is the best way to determine guilt or innocence.   ☑ SA   ☐ A   ☐ N   ☐ D   ☐ SD

    2. Juries usually make good decisions.   ☐ SA   ☑ A   ☐ N   ☐ D   ☐ SD

    3. Most jury awards are too large.   ☐ SA   ☐ A   ☐ N   ☐ D   ☑ SD

    4. Juries should be replaced with panels of judges.   ☐ SA   ☐ A   ☐ N   ☑ D   ☐ SD

8. Examine the results from the second stage of item analysis for the attitude item shown below. Do the data indicate that the item is working correctly? Explain.

    Item: Juries sometimes need to make complex decisions.

Response	SA	A	N	D	SD
Tallies for the 12 with the highest total scores:	////// //	////		/	
Tallies for the 12 with the lowest total scores:	//////	//////	/		/

9. Examine the results from the second stage of item analysis for the attitude item shown below. Do the data indicate that the item is working correctly? Explain.

Item: Most jurors carefully consider the evidence presented.

Response	SA	A	N	D	SD
Tallies for the 12 with the highest total scores:	////// /	/////	/		
Tallies for the 12 with the lowest total scores:		///	/	//////	///

10. If you have written questionnaire items, conduct think-alouds using at least two individuals. Did the think-alouds give you insight into how the items work? Explain. Did they help you identify flawed items? Explain.

Notes:

Chapter 7

Preparing a Questionnaire for Administration

After you have written items based on your research objectives, had them reviewed by others, tried them out with respondents who will not be in your main study, and revised them, you need to assemble them into a questionnaire.

Guideline 7.1   Write a descriptive title for the questionnaire.

The title should indicate very briefly the overall topic of the questionnaire. If you will be surveying individuals who are interested in the topic, the title may grab their attention and increase your response rate. Example 7.1.1 is the title for a survey on the health of new mothers. It is poor because it is not sufficiently descriptive — in fact, the key term in it, "CAREDATA," is jargon whose precise meaning is known only to those working in the organization conducting the survey.

Example 7.1.1

Title for a questionnaire on the health of new mothers:

CAREDATA Survey

Improved Version of Example 7.1.1

Mothers' Health Survey

The titles in Example 7.1.2 all describe very briefly the overall topics of their respective questionnaires.

Example 7.1.2

Examples of questionnaire titles:

Marriage Relationship Inventory

Long-Term Effects of War Experience Survey

Questionnaire on Grief Reactions to a Death

Guideline 7.2   Write an introduction to the questionnaire.

If your questionnaire will be mailed, it is customary to introduce it in a cover letter. If it will not be mailed, the introduction may be placed on the questionnaire immediately below the title. The introduction should be as brief as possible while covering the elements described below.

At a minimum, the introduction should indicate the purpose of the questionnaire and include an appeal for the respondents to answer the items. Examples 7.2.1 and 7.2.2 contain these two elements. Notice the use of first- and second-person pronouns ("we," "you," and "I"), which personalize it.

Example 7.2.1

First part of the introduction to a questionnaire:

We are conducting a survey of your satisfaction with the health care services you receive as a member of your health insurance plan. I am requesting your help to make this effort a success. Only a small random sample of our members has been selected to receive this survey. Therefore, your response is very important.

Example 7.2.2

First part of the introduction to a questionnaire:

We appreciated the opportunity to repair your bicycle on July 14. Because you are a valued customer, your views regarding the service you received are extremely important to us.

If the responses will be anonymous, emphasize this point in the introduction. Example 7.2.3 shows how this might be expressed.

Example 7.2.3

Be assured that your responses are **strictly confidential**. You are not being asked to provide your name on the questionnaire, so **all responses are anonymous**.

Also, consider using these other features in the introduction to your questionnaire:

- If there will be direct benefit to the respondent, indicate what it will be (for example, "Your responses will help us improve the health care services you receive.").
- Provide an estimate of how long it will take the respondent to answer the questions (for example, "only a few minutes" or "no longer than 10 minutes").
- If the questionnaire is to be returned by mail, indicate that a postage-paid reply envelope is enclosed.

- Express thanks near the end of the introduction (for example, "Thank you for taking the time to complete the questionnaire. We need and value your opinions." *or* "Thank you for helping us better understand how we are doing so that we can meet your needs.").
- End the introduction with a complimentary closing (for example, "Sincerely"), a signature, and a signature block that indicates the researcher's position within the organization (for example, "Jones E. Doe, Vice President and General Manager, Quality Assurance Division" *or* "Jane E. Jones, Doctoral Candidate in Psychology, Temple University").

Guideline 7.3   Group the items by content, and provide a subtitle for each group.

Grouping by content and providing a subtitle for each group of items helps respondents understand the organization of the questionnaire and breaks the task of answering the items on a long questionnaire into shorter, more manageable tasks. In addition, by grouping items according to their content, respondents do not have to jump back and forth mentally among topics. Example 7.3.1 shows the subtitles used in a questionnaire on satisfaction with health care services. Under each subtitle, there were 5 to 10 items. Note that the last group of items is labeled "About You and Your Family." The questions under this subtitle are demographic questions (background questions on age, marital status, income, and so on). They are placed at the end, as recommended in Chapter 3 of this book.

Example 7.3.1

Subtitles used for groups of items in a questionnaire:

About Your Selection of a Health Plan

About Your Primary Care Physician

About Specialists

About Prescription Drugs

About Preventive Service

About Customer Service

About You and Your Family

Guideline 7.4   Within each group of items, place items with the same format together.

Within each group of items dealing with similar content (see Guideline 7.3), group items by item type. That is, group together all "yes–no" questions, group together all open-ended questions, and so on.

Guideline 7.5   At the end of the questionnaire, indicate what respondents should do next.

If a questionnaire will be administered in a group setting, indicate whether respondents should wait quietly for others to finish or should turn in their questionnaires as soon as they have finished. Also indicate whether they are free to leave the room when they have finished. This will eliminate the need for those who finish early to ask questions about what they are to do, which may disturb those who have not finished responding to the questionnaire.

If questionnaires are to be mailed back by individual respondents, remind them of the postage-paid envelope you provided. Also, give the return address at the end of the questionnaire in case they misplace the return envelope.

Guideline 7.6   Prepare an informed consent form, if needed.

Many funding agencies and sponsoring organizations require researchers to obtain informed consent in writing from potential respondents. If you need to create a form to obtain their consent, check with the agency or organization to obtain their guidelines for creating such a form. Most consent forms contain the following elements:[1]

- The title of the research project.
- The name, address, and phone number of the principal investigator.
- The purpose of the research.
- The possible risks, discomfort, or harm that might result from participation.
- The possible benefits that might accrue from participation.
- Whether the responses will remain confidential and, if so, what steps will be taken to maintain their confidentiality.
- A space for the potential respondents to sign indicating they understand that they may withdraw their consent at any time without penalty or loss.

---

[1] Ask an appropriate administrator for a detailed description of the elements to be included. Also, request samples of consent forms that have been approved previously by the funding agency and/or the institution. You may be able to use these as models while you write a form for your research.

- The name, address, and phone number of the person respondents should contact in the future if they have any questions or realize at a later date that they have been harmed by their participation in the research.
- Spaces for the respondent to sign and date the informed consent form.

Guideline 7.7   If the questionnaire will be mailed to respondents, avoid having your correspondence look like junk mail.

If the envelope that you use to send the questionnaire looks like it contains junk mail, many potential respondents may not even open it. If you are not mailing very many questionnaires, consider printing the recipients' names and addresses on the envelopes rather than applying labels with this information. Using a first-class stamp instead of a preprinted bulk rate insignia will make it look more important and personal. Finally, consider printing a "teaser" on the envelope such as, "Your opinions will help us improve your child's school." Whether to use a teaser and what it should say should be considered carefully since there is the danger that an inappropriate teaser may turn off potential respondents, leading them to discard the envelope without opening it.

Guideline 7.8   If the questionnaire will be mailed, consider including a token reward.

Many researchers have increased response rates by attaching a new dollar bill to the front of each questionnaire. This grabs the attention of potential respondents and communicates indirectly that the questionnaire is designed to collect important information that is seriously needed. In addition, some respondents may feel guilty if they keep the dollar but do not fill out the questionnaire. If you use this technique, mention in your cover letter that the dollar is merely a "token" of your appreciation since it is certainly not enough to constitute payment for their efforts. Other tokens you might consider are coins and postage stamps.

Guideline 7.9   If the questionnaire will be mailed, write a follow-up letter.

If you mail questionnaires, you will almost certainly have nonrespondents —in fact, you may have a large percentage of nonrespondents. Typically, anywhere from 40% to 80% of those contacted by mail will not respond to the first mailing. You can usually substantially reduce the rate of nonresponse by means of a follow-up letter indicating that you know the respondents are busy but intend to return the completed questionnaire. The letter should also remind recipients why the research is important and that their responses are important to the success of the research project. Finally, it should ask the respondents to ignore the follow-up letter if they have already mailed back their questionnaires.

Guideline 7.10   If the questionnaire will be administered in person, consider preparing written instructions for the administrator.

This guideline is especially important if you will not be the person administering the questionnaire. For example, suppose you will have a sample of teachers throughout the country administer a questionnaire on recycling to middle-school students. Your written instructions might include a request for the teacher to withhold any class discussion of recycling until after the students have completed the questionnaires. In addition, you should include instructions on the types of help the teachers are permitted to give students (for instance, you might tell them in the instructions that teachers may read items aloud if students are having difficulty) and the types of help that are not permitted (for example, suggesting answers to students). In addition, you probably should instruct the teacher to read aloud the introduction and directions on the questionnaire to the students. Remember, many people ignore introductory material and directions unless they are called to their attention. Finally, don't forget to end your instructions with a thank you to the teachers for their help in making the data collection effort a success.

Exercise for Chapter 7

1. Comment on the adequacy of each of the following titles for questionnaires:

"Reactions Survey Questionnaire"

"Safe-Sex Practices Questionnaire"

"Campus Food Service Survey"

2. At a minimum, the introduction to a questionnaire should contain what two elements?

3. When responses will be anonymous, should the introduction to the questionnaire emphasize this point?

4. Should the items *first* be grouped by content *or* by item type?

5. Should the subtitles in a questionnaire indicate the content of each group of items (for example, quality of the food, cost of the food, and so on) *or* the types of items (yes-no items, multiple-choice items, and so on)?

6. Should a return address be given at the end of a questionnaire that is to be mailed back in addition to a postage-paid envelope? Why? Why not?

7. How might you make an envelope that contains a questionnaire look personal and important?

8. Why should you prepare a follow-up letter for mailed questionnaires?

9. If you have developed a questionnaire, write an introduction for it using the suggestions provided under Guideline 7.2.

Notes:

Chapter 8

Selecting a Sample of Respondents

When you write the objectives for your questionnaire (see Chapter 1), you should have a specific population in mind. A *population* is the group in which you are interested. It may be small, such as all social workers in a town, or large, such as all social workers in the nation. If you survey all members of a population (and they all participate in the study), you are conducting a *census*—that is, a count or survey of all members of a population. When populations are large, we often draw just a *sample* of its members, administer the questionnaire to them, and infer that what we learn about the sample is also true of the population. In this chapter, we will consider and evaluate basic methods of sampling.[1]

Guideline 8.1 Identify the accessible population.

While the *population* is the group a researcher is interested in, the *accessible population* is the group to which she has access. Consider, for example, a researcher who wishes to survey a sample of all accountants in the United States (her *population*) with a questionnaire, but she has access to only the mailing lists of the Association of Women Accountants and the Association of Government Accountants. The accountants who are on the mailing lists of these organizations constitute her *accessible population*— those to whom she has access. Notice that even though she wants to study all accountants (a *census*), she will be able to study only a sample of them — the accessible population. Since *sampling bias* results when some members of the population have a greater chance of being selected (such as female and government accountants in our example) than other members of the population (such as male and nongovernment accountants), her sample will be *biased*. Because biased samples can produce misleading results, many statisticians warn against attempting to generalize from a biased sample to the population. At best, any generalizations from biased samples should be made with considerable caution.

Of course, sometimes researchers have access to all members of the population in which they are interested. For example, the executive of a large corporation might be interested in the opinions of all salespeople who are employees of the corporation. Presumably, all of the salespeople are accessible to

---

[1] This chapter provides a discussion of only those methods of sampling most likely to be used by beginning researchers. Statistical methods for evaluating inferences from samples to populations are discussed in Chapter 12 and Appendix B.

the executive; thus, the population of interest is identical to the accessible population.

When the accessible population is very large, researchers often deliberately draw just a sample to study. A properly drawn sample *from the accessible population* will permit sound generalizations *to the accessible population*, even if the accessible population is a biased subgroup of the population of interest. For example, a properly drawn sample of members of the Association of Women Accountants and the Association of Government Accountants will permit sound generalizations to all members of these associations (the accessible population), even though it will produce results of dubious value in generalizing to all accountants in the United States (the population of interest).

The following guidelines will assist you in deciding how to sample from an accessible population.

Guideline 8.2   Avoid using samples of convenience.

A *sample of convenience* (also known as an *accidental sample*) consists of respondents who are conveniently available for participation in a study. For example, much of the research published in academic journals is conducted by professors who use students who are convenient to them (such as students in their classes) as respondents.[2] Of course, such samples are biased in favor of those who take the types of courses that the professor teaches, prefer to take courses at the times the professor usually teaches, have enrolled in the university at which the professor teaches, and so on.

Samples of convenience are, by definition, biased samples because they do not give each member of a population an equal chance of being selected. (Those who are convenient have a high chance of being selected while those who are not convenient have a low chance.) Thus, samples of convenience should be avoided. The studies in which they are used usually should be labeled as *pilot studies* in reports. Pilot studies are ones in which methods and materials such as questionnaires are initially tried out prior to their use in more definitive studies. The main justification for conducting pilot studies is that they may help researchers refine their methods and materials (such as identifying and removing ambiguities in questionnaire items). The main justification for publishing the results of pilot studies is that they may contain promising leads that might be pursued by other researchers who have the resources to obtain better samples.

---

[2] Note that a *sample of convenience* is *not* necessarily equivalent to an *accessible population*. For instance, a psychology professor may have access to all students who are psychology majors at her university (her accessible population) but may use only those students in her class as respondents because it is convenient to do so.

Guideline 8.3   Simple random sampling is a desirable method of sampling.

A simple random sample is obtained by giving each member of the population an equal chance of being selected. This can be done by putting the names of all members of the population on slips of paper, mixing them thoroughly, and drawing names. For larger populations, it is more efficient to use a table of random numbers. An abbreviated table is shown in Appendix C on page 138 of this book. To use the table, each member of the population must be given a "number name." The number of digits in each member's number name must be the same as the number of digits in the population size. For example, if there are 900 people in a population (note that 900 contains 3 digits) each member of the population must be given a number name with three digits. One person should be given the number name "000," another should be renamed "001," another "002," and so on. It does not matter who is given which number name since we are only renaming at this point — we are not yet selecting a sample. Examples 8.3.1 and 8.3.2 both illustrate how to select a simple random sample using the table in Appendix C.[3]

Example 8.3.1

To draw a simple random sample from a population of 400, a researcher renamed each member with a three-digit name starting with 000. Without looking, she put her finger on Table 1 on page 138 of this book, and it happened to land on the first digit in row # 1, which begins with the three-digit number "210," so the person named 210 was selected. Continuing to the right, the next three-digit number is "498." Since no one was named 498 (remember, there are only 400 members of the population), this number selected no one. Continuing to the right, the next three-digit number is "088," so person number 088 was selected. She continued in this manner until she had a simple random sample of 250 respondents.

Example 8.3.2

To draw a simple random sample from a population of 5,599, a researcher renamed each member with a four-digit name starting with 0000. Without looking, he put his finger on Table 1 on page 138 of this book, and it happened to land on the first digit in row # 22, which begins with the four-digit number "3780" (ignoring the vertical space between the digits 8 and 0), so the person named 3780 was selected. Continuing to the right, the next four-digit number is "6371." Since no one was named 6371 (remember, there are only 5,599 members of the population), this number selected no one. Continuing to the right, the next four-digit number is "2652," so person number 2652 was selected. He continued in this manner until he had a simple random sample of 600 respondents.

---

[3] Books containing tables of random numbers with more numbers than those in Appendix C can be obtained in most academic libraries. Also, computer programs can be used to generate a random selection.

Since simple random sampling gives everyone in the population an equal chance of being selected, it yields an unbiased sample of the population. Keep in mind that if your *accessible population* (see Guideline 8.1) is a biased subgroup of the population of interest, simple random sampling will yield an unbiased sample of only the accessible population—not an unbiased sample of the entire population of interest.

Guideline 8.4   Systematic sampling is an acceptable method of sampling.

In systematic sampling, every n^{th} person is selected. For example, if $n = 2$, then every second person is selected; if $n = 3$, every third person is selected; and so on. When using this method, it is highly desirable to select from an alphabetical list of the population. Otherwise, you may fall prey to someone's ordering of the list. For example, a teacher may have put a high achiever next to a low achiever, next to a high achiever, and so on in the hope that high achievers would help low achievers with their classwork. If you pick every other student from this teacher's class, you could end up with a sample of only high achievers or only low achievers. Using an alphabetical list ensures that no one has tampered with the ordering of the list. Finally, you must go all the way through the alphabet since different national-origin groups tend to concentrate at different points in the alphabet. When conducted as described here, systematic sampling produces a sample that is essentially as good as one obtained by using simple random sampling.[4]

Guideline 8.5   Stratification may reduce sampling errors.

We stratify by dividing a population into strata (subgroups). For example, it is common to stratify on the basis of gender. To stratify, we separate the names of the women from the names of the men. Then we draw separate samples of men and women. For example, if we draw 10% of the men and then draw 10% of the women separately using the technique of simple random sampling (see Guideline 8.3), we have drawn what is known as a *stratified random sample*. On the other hand, if we draw 10% of the men and then draw 10% of the women separately

---

[4] The formal definition of *random sampling* is a procedure in which all are given an equal and independent chance of being selected. While *systematic sampling* gives all an equal chance of being selected, it does not give them an independent chance. That is, once the first person is selected in systematic sampling, all others are selected automatically (such as every third one). Thus, systematic sampling does not meet the full formal definition of *random* and should not be called *random*.

using the technique of systematic sampling (see Guideline 8.4), we have drawn what is known as a *stratified systematic sample.*

Sampling errors are defined as random or chance errors that are caused by random sampling. By using simple random sampling, for example, we might, purely by chance, get a disproportionately large number of men — a sampling error. By stratifying on gender as described above, we preclude the possibility of this particular type of sampling error. Note that it is essential to use *equal percentages*—not equal numbers—when drawing stratified samples. For instance, if there are 900 women and 400 men in a population, drawing an equal percentage of each will maintain the balance in favor of women. That is, if we draw 10% of the women, we will get 90 women and if we draw 10% of the men, we will get 40 men. Thus, this sample is proportionately representative of the gender composition of the population.

Researchers often find that place of residence is a useful stratification variable since people with similar incomes, religious beliefs, language preferences, and so on often live near each other. Thus, if you draw the same percentage of people who reside in each voting precinct in a city, you will guarantee that all areas of the city (those with rich and those with poor residents, those with large numbers of immigrants and those with small numbers of immigrants, and so on) will be represented in about the right proportions.

Guideline 8.6   Consider using random cluster sampling when every member of a population belongs to a group.

Cluster sampling may be used if each member of a population belongs to a pre-existing group (called a *cluster*). Clusters usually have leaders. For example, all members of the Girl Scouts belong to a cluster (a troop) that has a leader. For this population, you could draw names of troops at random rather than drawing names of individual Girl Scouts at random. This would give you a random sample of the clusters. You will probably find it more convenient to contact just the leaders of the selected troops than to contact individual Girl Scouts. In addition, if you can convince the troop leaders of the importance of your questionnaire research, you probably will find that they will help you get the cooperation of the Girl Scouts in filling out your questionnaires.

In school settings, the obvious clusters are class sections — each of which has a leader — the teacher. With the approval of school administrators, teachers can distribute the questionnaires, collect them, and return them to the researcher.

Unfortunately, cluster sampling has a disadvantage. To get precise results using this technique, you must use a large number of clusters. To see why this is so, suppose you randomly selected five class sections from a university with an average size of 25 students per class, giving you a total of 125 respondents (5 classes times 25 students yields 125 students). Even if 125 is a reasonable size for your sample (sample size will be discussed later in this chapter), five clusters may not be. For example, the five class sections drawn at random might contain one beginning English class, two advanced math classes, and two teacher education classes. Thus, it may not contain a single art class, engineering class, business or finance class, and so on. To get around this problem, you need to draw a large number of clusters.[5] As a very rough rule, use at least 30 clusters—more if you have the resources to do so.

Guideline 8.7   Consider using multistage sampling to select respondents from large populations.

In multistage sampling, we first draw large clusters and then draw smaller and smaller clusters or individuals. To get a good sample using this technique, the selections should be made randomly at each stage. Example 8.7.1 illustrates two-stage sampling.

Example 8.7.1

The population consisted of all registered nurses employed by hospitals in California. In the first stage, the researcher obtained a master list of all hospitals and drew a stratified random sample of hospitals in urban, suburban, and rural areas. She then contacted the administrators of the selected hospitals and obtained lists of all registered nurses employed by them. In the second stage, she drew a simple random sample of the nurses employed by the selected hospitals.

Notice in Example 8.7.1 that the researcher needed to come up with only a list of all hospitals in various regions of California in the first stage. It was not necessary to obtain a list of individual nurses until the second stage, which was relatively easy at that point since she needed only the names of those working at selected hospitals.

Example 8.7.2 illustrates three-stage sampling.

Example 8.7.2

The population consisted of all public high school students in Texas. In the first stage, the researcher drew a simple random sample of all public high schools in Texas. In the second stage, he stratified on the basis of grade level (freshman, sophomore, etc.) and drew a stratified random sample of homeroom sections

---

[5] Some mathematical statisticians recommend that the number of clusters should equal the number of respondents you desire. For example, if you need 125 respondents, they suggest you draw 125 *clusters* and treat the average response of each cluster as a single score, in effect, giving you a sample size of 125.

separately from each grade level. Within each homeroom selected in the second stage, he drew a simple random sample of individual students.

Guideline 8.8   Consider the importance of getting precise results when determining sample size.

When we say that the results of questionnaire research are *very precise*, we are saying they are relatively free of random sampling errors. We can increase precision by increasing sample size. For some research problems, we can easily tolerate an error of a few percentage points. For example, in a survey on people's attitudes toward environmental laws, if we come within a few percentage points of the true answer in the population based on a sample of 1,000 respondents, we probably would be satisfied. On the other hand, when conducting a political poll just before a major election, many pollsters want to be more precise; thus, they use a sample of about 1,500 to get within about 1% of the truth. Deciding how large a sample should be depends largely on how precise your results need to be.

What we are talking about here is called a *margin of error*. For example, if your sample indicates that 55% approve of enacting stricter environmental laws and you have a margin of error of 3%, you can be confident that the true percentage that approves is somewhere between 52% and 58% (that is, 55% +/– 3% = 52% and 58%).

The Gallup Organization, publisher of many polls and *The Gallup Poll Monthly*, uses the guidelines in Table 8.8.1 to estimate the 95% margin of error. That is, you can be 95% confident that the true answer lies within the number of percentage points given. For example, if you can tolerate being off from the truth by up to about 7 to 11 percentage points 95% of the time (and being even farther off the other 5% of the time), you might consider using a sample of 100 respondents. Clearly, Table 8.8.1 will be useful when considering how large your sample should be. Use it to select a sample size that will give you roughly the amount of sampling error you are willing to tolerate.

Table 8.8.1   *Points to allow for 95% margins of error for various sample sizes*

Sample size	Number of percentage points to allow
100	7 to 11
200	5 to 8
400	4 to 6
600	3 to 5
750	3 to 4
1,000	2 to 4

Note that in Chapter 12, we will consider how to compute the precise margins of error for your specific results. At this point, we are considering Table 8.8.1 to make a rough estimate of how large your sample should be.[6]

Guideline 8.9 Remember that using a large sample does not compensate for a bias in sampling.

You can obtain an unbiased sample by using simple random sampling, systematic sampling, stratified random sampling, stratified systematic sampling, random cluster sampling, or multistage random sampling, all of which were described earlier in this chapter. Obtaining an unbiased sample (one that gives everyone an equal chance of being selected) is the foremost consideration in sampling.

Using a large sample does not compensate for having a bias in sampling. To see that this is so, let's consider an extreme example. Suppose you want to estimate the opinions of all students (your population) on the food service at the cafeteria on campus. Instead of drawing a random sample of all students, you go directly to the entrance of the cafeteria to distribute your questionnaires. You even set up a rule for yourself that you will hand a questionnaire to every 20th person who enters the cafeteria with a personal appeal to them to answer your questions. But you have a biased sample, don't you? Notice that those who enter the cafeteria have a 1 in 20 chance of being selected while those who do not enter the cafeteria have no chance of being selected. By definition, the sample is biased since an equal chance was not accorded everyone in the population. In addition, it's quite possible that those who do not go to the cafeteria think that the food is prepared poorly and is expensive, while those who go to the cafeteria think the food service is quite adequate. Thus, even if you stand at the entrance day and night for weeks on end to get a huge sample (say, 3,000), you will learn only the opinions of those who think it is adequate.

Guideline 8.10 Consider sampling nonrespondents to get information on the nature of a bias.

A major problem in questionnaire research results from potential respondents not bothering or refusing to respond. This is especially likely to occur when questionnaires are mailed to them. The danger here is that nonrespondents may be systematically different from those who respond. To check on this

---

[6] Of course, we often report averages instead of percentages in questionnaire research. Even if you will be reporting averages, Table 8.8.1 is still useful in giving you a very rough idea of how large your sample should be. Obtaining margins of error for averages is considered in Chapter 12.

possibility, it is desirable to contact a small random sample of the nonrespondents in person or by phone to elicit responses to your questions by reading the questions to them.[7] Then, you can use this small sample to represent all the nonrespondents. If the information they provide is similar to that provided by those who mailed back the questionnaire, you may conclude that the bias did not have a great effect on the results you obtained by mailing your questionnaire. If they are substantially different, you may want to view the main body of your data (obtained using questionnaires that were mailed back) with considerable caution.[8]

Exercise for Chapter 8

1. Briefly describe the difference between a population of interest and an accessible population.

2. How should you usually label studies in which samples of convenience are used?

3. Suppose you wanted to draw a simple random sample from a population with 3,452 members. If you start at the beginning of row 25 in Table 1 on page 138, what are the numbers of the first two members drawn?

4. Suppose you wanted to draw a simple random sample from a population with 818 members. If you start at the beginning of row 14 in Table 1 on page 138, what are the numbers of the first two members drawn?

5. What is the name of the method of sampling in which every n^{th} person is drawn?

---

[7] You may recall from Chapter 1 that contacting potential respondents by phone or in person usually yields a higher response rate than mailed surveys. Thus, these methods are recommended for contacting a small sample of those who did not respond to a mailed questionnaire.

[8] It is also possible to mathematically adjust the data for those who responded by mail based on the small sample of initial nonrespondents who were contacted in person or by phone. The statistical issues regarding this type of adjustment and the mathematics for making an adjustment are beyond the scope of this book.

6. Why is it recommended that you draw from an alphabetical list if you use systematic sampling?

7. If you draw 20% of the freshmen, 20% of the sophomores, 20% of the juniors, and 20% of the seniors using simple random sampling to select separately from each subgroup, you are using what type of sampling?

8. Briefly explain the advantage of stratified random sampling over simple random sampling.

9. Write a very brief example of random cluster sampling other than the examples given in this chapter.

10. Write a very brief example of multistage sampling other than the examples given in this chapter.

11. According to this chapter, if you are willing to tolerate only about 2 to 4 percentage points for your margin of error, what size sample should you use?

12. Does using a very large sample compensate for a bias in the sampling procedure? Explain.

13. Why should you contact in person or by phone a small random sample of those who do not respond to a mailed questionnaire?

Chapter 9

Preparing Statistical Tables and Figures

After the questionnaires have been returned, you will need to analyze the data. In this chapter, we will consider how to use the data you collect to prepare statistical *tables* (organized sets of values) and *figures* (drawings based on the values in tables).

Guideline 9.1   Prepare a table of frequencies.

If you will be reporting separately on each questionnaire item, the first step in the analysis is to determine how many respondents marked each choice. Example 9.1.1 shows the numbers that marked each choice in two of the items in a questionnaire for evaluating a professor's performance. Since the values in it are organized and ordered, it is called a statistical table. Note that the symbol for *number of respondents* is the letter N (if you conducted a census) or n (if you surveyed only a sample). Sometimes researchers use the letter f for *frequency of response* instead of N or n.

Example 9.1.1

Table 9.1.1   *Student evaluations for Professor Doe's research class (N = 25)*

Rating	**Excellent**	**Very Good**	**Fair**	**Poor**	**Very Poor**
Item 1: Encourages student participation in class					
N	5	2	12	4	2
Item 2: Is available to help outside class					
N	13	9	2	0	1

Comparing the frequencies of response to the two items in Example 9.1.1 indicates clearly that the professor has higher ratings overall on the second item than the first.

The ordered sets of frequencies in Example 9.1.1 are called *frequency distributions*. They show how the frequencies are distributed. For Item 1, the distribution is roughly *symmetrical*, with most of the respondents clustered in the center and roughly equal numbers spread out equally far on both sides. For Item 2, the distribution is *skewed*. A skewed distribution is one in which most respondents cluster in one area with a small proportion far off on one side or the other. When the small proportion is off to the right (as it is for Item 2), we say that the distribution is *skewed to the right*. Obviously, if the small proportion is to the left, we say it is *skewed to the left*. The terms *symmetrical* and *skewed* are helpful when describing distributions within a research report. In addition, whether a distribution is symmetrical or skewed has important implications, as explained in the next chapter.

For attitude scales, we usually score each item and sum the scores on the items to get a total score for each respondent. The total score indicates the degree to which a respondent has a positive attitude toward the object of the scale.[1] When analyzing the results using such a scale, the first step in the analysis is to determine how many respondents earned each total score and to organize the data into a table such as the one shown in Example 9.1.2. Note that the scores have been grouped into intervals such as 67–71, 62–66, and so on. This was done to keep the table from becoming too large.

Example 9.1.2

Table 9.1.2 *Distribution of attitude scores*

Score Interval	Number of respondents
67–71	2
62–66	1
57–61	2
52–56	4
47–51	6
42–46	7
37–41	8
32–36	5
27–31	2
22–26	0
17–21	2
12–16	1
	$N = 40$

Inspection of Table 9.1.2 shows clearly that most respondents clustered between scores of 32 and 56, with a scattering farther out on both sides. Thus, this table will give readers of a report on the research a very good indication of how the scores are distributed.

---

[1] Writing attitude scales is discussed in Chapter 4, and scoring them is illustrated under Guideline 6.7 in Chapter 6.

Guideline 9.2   Consider calculating percentages and arranging them in a table with the frequencies.

As you know, a percentage is calculated by dividing the part by the whole and multiplying by 100. For instance, if 30 out of 75 respondents rate a product as being excellent, then 40% rate it as excellent (that is, $30/75 = .40 \times 100 = 40\%$).

Example 9.2.1 shows the distributions in Example 9.1.1 with the frequencies (number of respondents) supplemented with percentages.

Example 9.2.1

Table 9.2.1   *Student evaluations for Professor Doe's research class with percentages (N = 25)*

Rating	Excellent	Very Good	Fair	Poor	Very Poor
Item 1: Encourages student participation in class					
N	5	2	12	4	2
Percentage	20.0%	8.0%	48.0%	16.0%	8.0%
Item 2: Is available to help outside class					
N	13	9	2	0	1
Percentage	52.0%	36.0%	8.0%	0.0%	4.0%

A major advantage of percentages over frequencies is that they make the results comparable across two or more groups of unequal size. Consider Example 9.2.2. Since the group of women has 40 respondents, while the group of men has 80 respondents, comparison of the groups using frequencies can be confusing. However, percentages are not confusing since a percentage indicates the number of respondents *per 100*. That is, for both the women and the men, a percentage indicates the number of respondents who would be in each score interval *if both groups had 100 respondents who were distributed in the same way*. For example, if there were 100 women, the percentage of 5.0 for the interval from 67 to 71 tells us that there would be 5 women in this interval.

Notice that the advantage of percentages over frequencies is illustrated dramatically in Example 9.2.2 where a comparison of the frequencies for the women and the men is confusing because there are more men in virtually every score interval, but a comparison of the percentages makes it clear that the two distributions are identical since each score interval has the same percentage of women and men.

A common misconception among beginning researchers is that all groups of respondents must be equal in number in order to make legitimate comparisons of the groups. In light of the previous two paragraphs, you can see that this is not true.

Of course, two distributions that have identical percentages are very rarely found; they are shown here for instructional purposes only. Example 9.2.3 shows a more realistic table containing percentages. Notice the percentages are shown in a larger font than the numbers of cases (*n*) to emphasize the percentages. Comparison of the percentages shows that, overall, the men are somewhat younger than the women.

Example 9.2.2

Table 9.2.2   *Distributions of attitude scores for women and men*

Score Interval	Number of respondents **Women**	Percentage of respondents **Women**	Number of respondents **Men**	Percentage of respondents **Men**
67–71	2	5.0	4	5.0
62–66	1	2.5	2	2.5
57–61	2	5.0	4	5.0
52–56	4	10.0	8	10.0
47–51	6	15.0	12	15.0
42–46	7	17.5	14	17.5
37–41	8	20.0	16	20.0
32–36	5	12.5	10	12.5
27–31	2	5.0	4	5.0
22–26	0	0.0	0	0.0
17–21	2	5.0	4	5.0
12–16	1	2.5	2	2.5
	$N = 40$	100.0%	$N = 80$	100.0%

Example 9.2.3

Table 9.2.3   *Ages of respondents by gender*

Age	Women ($n = 830$)	Men ($n = 723$)
18 years and under	4.8% ($n = 40$)	8.7% ($n = 63$)
19–24 years	9.9% ($n = 82$)	13.3% ($n = 96$)
25–34 years	18.2% ($n = 151$)	25.4% ($n = 184$)
35–44 years	22.8% ($n = 189$)	19.4% ($n = 140$)
45–54 years	20.0% ($n = 166$)	15.4% ($n = 111$)
55–64 years	13.7% ($n = 114$)	13.8% ($n = 100$)
65–74 years	5.3% ($n = 44$)	2.6% ($n = 19$)
75 years and over	5.3% ($n = 44$)	1.4% ($n = 10$)
Total	100.0%	100.0%

Guideline 9.3   For nominal data, consider constructing a bar graph.

Nominal data are naming data. For example, if we ask respondents to name their gender, they name either "male" or "female." Other examples of nominal data are having respondents name the country in which they were born, name the political party to which they belong, and name their major in college. Notice that nominal data does *not* lend itself to being translated into a set of sequenced numerical scores. That is, it would defy logic to award scores to students' majors such as English = 0, Psychology = 1, Math = 3, and so on. There is no basis on which we could all agree for giving Psychology a higher score than English.

For nominal data, the usual method of analysis is to compute percentages. These may be presented in a table as shown in Example 9.3.1. They also may be presented in a bar graph, as shown in Example 9.3.2. Bar graphs may contain either vertical or horizontal bars. Note that a drawing that presents data is called a *statistical figure*.

Example 9.3.1

Table 9.3.1   *Sources of fear reported by fifth-grade children (n = 100)*

Violence	Death	Animals	School	Other
70% (*n* = 70)	50% (*n* = 50)	40% (*n* = 40)	20% (*n* = 20)	10% (*n* = 10)

Note: Each child was permitted to name more than one source of fear. Thus, percentages do not sum to 100%.

Example 9.3.2

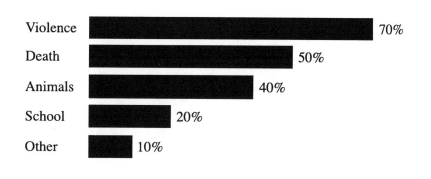

Figure 9.3.2   *Sources of fear reported by fifth-grade children (n = 100)*

It is important to note that each table and figure should be given a number and a title (called a *caption*). Also, according to conventional standards in the social and behavioral sciences, tables are labeled *above* the table while figures are labeled *below* the figure. These conventions are followed throughout this chapter.

Guideline 9.4   Consider preparing a histogram to display a distribution of scores.

A *histogram* is a figure that contains vertical bars. It is useful for displaying the distribution of scores or the percentages based on the scores. Example 9.4.1 shows a histogram for the percentages of women in each age group in Example 9.2.3.

Example 9.4.1

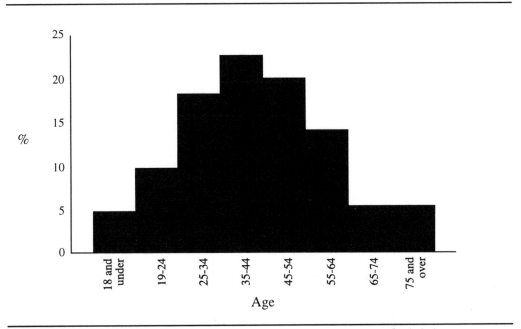

Figure 9.4.1   *Histogram of women's ages based on Example 9.2.3*

Guideline 9.5   Consider preparing polygons if distributions of scores are to be compared.

A *polygon* consists of connected dots. Example 9.5.1 shows a polygon that corresponds to the histogram in Example 9.4.1. Notice that in a polygon, dashed lines are used at both ends to make it look like it is resting on the base.

Whether to use a histogram or polygon to present a single set of scores is a matter of personal preference. When presenting sets of scores for two or three groups, polygons are superior because they permit a drawing using different kinds of lines for each group on the same set of axes.[2] This is illustrated in Example 9.5.2, which is based on the percentages for women and men in Example 9.2.3.

Example 9.5.1

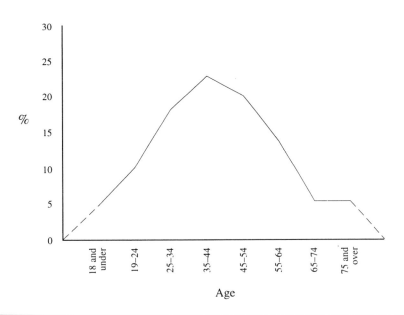

Figure 9.5.1   *Polygon showing women's ages*

Example 9.5.2

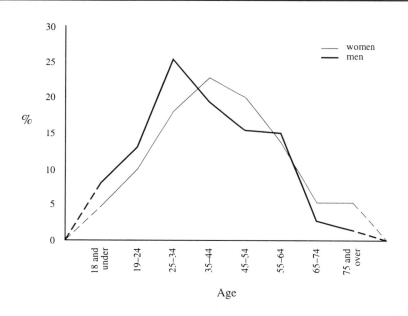

Figure 9.5.2   *Polygons showing women's and men's ages*

---

[2] Note that it is generally unsatisfactory to try to superimpose one set of bars on another to compare groups using histograms.

Concluding Comment

The choice between using a statistical table or a figure to present frequencies and percentages is largely a matter of personal choice. Generally, figures are more eye-catching, and many people find them easier to interpret than tables. A drawback to both tables and figures is that they consume more space than the statistical methods that we will explore in the next chapter.

Exercise for Chapter 9

1. What does the letter *f* stand for?

2. What does the letter *n* stand for?

3. What is the definition of a skewed distribution?

4. Briefly describe the major advantage of percentages over frequencies.

5. Briefly define the term *nominal data*, and give an example to illustrate your definition. Do *not* use the examples in this chapter as your example.

6. Calculate the percentages, rounded to one decimal place, for each score interval in the table on the next page and write them in the appropriate spaces.

Table for Question 6

Score Interval	Number of respondents	Percentage of respondents
43-45	4	
40-42	7	
37-39	3	
34-36	9	
31-33	18	
28-30	22	
25-27	8	
22-24	6	
19-21	5	
16-18	4	
13-15	2	
	$N =$	

7. Is the distribution in the table for question 6 clearly skewed? Explain.

8. Prepare a histogram based on the score intervals and percentages in question 6. Plan it so that it fits neatly in the space below. You may want to draw it on graph paper and attach it in the space.

9. Is the histogram you prepared for question 8 an example of a statistical table *or* an example of a statistical figure?

10. Did you remember to give the histogram you prepared for question 8 both a number and a title (caption)?

11. How does a polygon differ from a histogram?

12. When is a polygon clearly superior to a histogram?

Chapter 10

Describing Averages and Variability

The statistics described in this chapter are designed to provide very concise descriptions of distributions of scores. For example, a distribution might be described with just two values—one for its *average*, which indicates the location of the center of a distribution, and another for its *variability*, which indicates by how much the scores differ from one another.

Guideline 10.1   Use the median as the average for ordinal data.

Ordinal data are rank order data. For example, an item might present foster child care workers with a list of potential problems and ask the workers to rank order them by giving a rank of "1" to the most important problem, a rank of "2" to the next most important one, and so on. You may recall that Guideline 2.13 suggests that you use ranking items sparingly, if at all. If you do use them, the appropriate way to summarize the responses is to compute the *median* for each characteristic that was ranked. The median is defined as the average that has half the cases above it and half the cases below it. Example 10.1.1 illustrates how to compute the median when you have an odd number of ranks.

Example 10.1.1

Nine foster child care workers were presented with a list of 7 problems and asked to rank them from 1 to 7, with a rank of 1 indicating the most important problem. These are the ranks that they gave for the problem of "maintaining discipline":

5, 7, 1, 2, 3, 2, 4, 5, 2

To calculate the median, first put the ranks in order from lowest to highest, as shown here:

1, 2, 2, 2, 3, 4, 5, 5, 7

Then count to the middle rank. Since there are nine ranks, the middle rank is the fifth one (with four ranks above it and four ranks below it). The arrow indicates that the fifth rank up from the bottom is 3. Hence, the median is 3. Put another way, the average respondent gave maintaining discipline a rank of 3.

1, 2, 2, 2, 3, 4, 5, 5, 7
⇧

When there is an even number of scores, count to the middle *two* scores, add them together and divide by two. In Example 10.1.2, there are eight ranks that have been put in order from low to high. The arrows show the two middle scores.

Example 10.1.2[1]

3, 4, 5, 5, 6, 7, 7, 7
⇧ ⇧

The median is 5 + 6 = 11/2 = 5.5

Guideline 10.2   Consider using the mean as the average for equal interval data.

Equal interval data[2] indicate where respondents are on a numerical scale that has equal intervals among the score points. Clearly, a ruler has equal intervals (that is, the distance between a 1 and a 2 on a ruler is the same as the distance between a 2 and a 3, and so on). Likewise, age is equal interval with the same amount of time between age 1 and age 2, between age 2 and age 3, and so on. (You may recall that you learned under Guideline 2.13 in Chapter 2, rank order data are *not* equal interval. To see this, consider three people who have ranks of 1, 2, and 3 on height. The first person may be only an inch taller than the second one, while the second one may be a foot taller than the third one. Thus, the distances between 1, 2, and 3 are *not* equal interval—they are ordinal. As you know from the first guideline in this chapter, you should use the median as the average for ordinal data.)

The *mean* is the most popular average for summarizing equal interval data. It is computed by summing the scores and dividing by the number of scores. For example, if five respondents to a survey reported their ages as 20, 21, 25, 29, and 31, the mean age is 20 + 21 + 25 + 29 + 31 = 126/5 = 25.2.

Most researchers treat the scores they get by using attitude scales as equal interval data. (See Guideline 6.7 in Chapter 6 to review how to score individual attitude items and sum the scores to get a total attitude score for each respondent.)

---

[1] Notice that one of the middle ranks is tied (that is, the two ranks of 5 are tied with each other). It used to be common to make a slight adjustment in the value of the median using a process called interpolation when there were ties in the middle. Since popular statistical computer programs do not make this adjustment, it has fallen into disuse.

[2] Statisticians distinguish between equal interval scales that have an absolute zero (which they call *ratio* scales) and equal interval scales that do not have such a zero (which they simply call *interval* scales). This distinction has no implications for our discussions in this book.

For these attitude scores: 55, 60, 76, and 80, the mean is 55 + 60 + 76 + 80 = 271/4 = 67.8.

Also, most researchers who analyze responses to Likert-type items (i.e., items with choices from "Strongly agree" to "Strongly disagree") consider the points along the continuum to be equal interval. For example, they consider the mental distance between "Strongly agree" and "Agree" to be about the same as the mental distance between "Strongly disagree" and "Disagree." Example 10.2.1 shows a shortcut for calculating the mean for such an item.

Example 10.2.1

A department chair was evaluated through use of a questionnaire completed by 14 members of the department faculty. One of the items is shown below. The first step in the analysis is to tally how many faculty members marked each choice.

Item: Demonstrates leadership in curricular development and revision.

	Very effective	Somewhat effective	Somewhat ineffective	Very ineffective
Score	3	2	1	0
Tallies (showing how many marked each)	////	/////	////	/

In order to compute the mean, we need the sum of the scores. A quick way to get the sum is to (a) multiply each score by the number of respondents marking it as shown in the bottom row of the following table, and (b) sum the products shown in bold (12 + 10 + 4 + 0 = 26). Since the mean is defined as the sum of the scores divided by the number of respondents, we simply divide 26 by 14 (the number of respondents) to get the mean of 1.86.

	Very effective	Somewhat effective	Somewhat ineffective	Very ineffective
Score	3	2	1	0
Number marking each (based on the tallies)	4	5	4	1
Products (multiply each score by the number marking that choice)	3 x 4 = 12	2 x 5 = 10	1 x 4 = 4	0 x 1 = 0

By following the procedure in Example 10.2.1, we can obtain the means for all the items on the evaluation questionnaire and arrange them in a table such as the one shown in Example 10.2.2. Comparing the means for the various items, we can identify the department chair's areas of strength and weakness, which makes it clear that she is strongest in terms of item 2 and weakest in terms of item 4.

Example 10.2.2

Table 10.2.2   *Means ratings on effectiveness of a department chair on a scale from 0 (very ineffective) to 3 (very effective)*

Item	Average (mean)
1. Demonstrates leadership in curricular development and revision	1.86
2. Demonstrates leadership in the recruitment, selection, and retention of highly qualified faculty	2.76
3. Schedules classes to maximize faculty and other resources	2.05
4. Is available to faculty and staff	1.40
5. Provides for effective function of the division office	2.33
6. Involves faculty, where appropriate, in department decision making	1.99

Guideline 10.3   Use the median as the average for highly skewed, equal interval data.

Equal interval data was defined under the previous guideline. Although the mean is the most popular average for summarizing equal interval data, it does not provide a good estimate of the average when the data form a highly skewed distribution. You learned in the last chapter that a *skewed distribution* is one in which a majority of the respondents have scores in one area but a minority have scores that are far above *or* far below that of the majority. Example 10.3.1 illustrates what we mean by a skewed distribution. The distribution in Table 10.3.1 is highly skewed since the vast majority (26 out of 30) have scores at the high end (in fact, they are all in the 90s) while a minority (4 out of 30) have very low scores (that is, scores of 22, 14, 10, and 10).

Example 10.3.1

Thirty high school students in a program for the academically gifted were administered a questionnaire on their attitudes toward higher education. The scores could range from 0 to 100. (*Note:* See Guideline 6.7 for information on scoring attitude scales.[3]) The distribution of their scores is shown in Table 10.3.1 on the next page. The *mean* of the scores equals 84.8, while the *median* equals 95.0.

---

[3] Attitude scales are usually assumed to yield equal interval data.

Table 10.3.1   *Distribution of attitude scores*

Score	Number obtaining each score
100	8
96	7
94	3
93	4
91	3
90	1
22	1
14	1
10	2

The distribution in Example 10.3.1 has two different averages — the mean (84.8) and the median (95.0). The difference exists because the mean is pulled in the direction of the skew (that is, toward the minority of the scores that lie far from the majority). In the example we are considering, the minority with low scores (such as the two respondents with a score of 10) has pulled down the mean. Which value is a better representation of the average of this distribution? Statisticians agree almost universally that the median (in this case, 95.0) is more representative of the average in a highly skewed distribution than the mean (in this case, 84.8).

If you haven't studied statistics before, it's easy to get lost, so let's briefly review the principles for selecting an average before we move on to another type of statistic. The three principles are:

1. Use the *median* as the average for ordinal data (rank order data).
2. Use the *mean* as the average for equal interval data that are roughly symmetrical (that is, a distribution that is not highly skewed).
3. Use the *median* as the average for equal interval data that are highly skewed.

Guideline 10.4   Use the range very sparingly as the measure of variability.

The term *variability* refers to the extent to which scores vary or differ from one another. For example, if everyone in a group of respondents has the same score, then the set of scores has no variability. If respondents' scores are very different from one another, then there is much variability. The *range* is a measure of variability based on the two most extreme scores. It is simply the highest score minus the lowest score.[4] For the scores (years of education completed) in Example 10.4.1, the range is $12 - 1 = 11$.

---

[4] Some researchers add 1 to the difference. Thus, for Example 10.4.1, they might report that the range is 12 $(12 - 1 + 1 = 12)$.

Example 10.4.1 *Years of education completed by respondents*

1, 9, 9, 9, 10, 10, 10, 11, 12, 12, 12, 12, 12, 12, 12, 12

As you can see in Example 10.4.1, there is relatively little variability among the scores since all but one respondent completed between 9 and 12 years of education. The range has been pulled up to 11 points by one *outlier* that is far from the rest of the group — the person who completed only one year of education.[5] This person has skewed the distribution. The fact that the range can be highly influenced by a tiny minority that is far from the main group of respondents in a distribution is a major weakness. Thus, the range is seldom used unless it is also accompanied by one of the other measures of variability described below.

Guideline 10.5   If the median has been selected as the average, use the interquartile range as the measure of variability.

The *interquartile range* is a modified version of the range. Specifically, it is the range of the middle 50% of the scores or ranks. The values in Example 10.5.1 are ranks assigned by 16 clinical psychologists in private practice to the choice "keeping records for tax purposes" in a list of 12 problems associated with the business aspects of private practice. A rank of 1 in the example indicates that a psychologist thinks that keeping records for tax purposes is the most important problem among those listed, a rank of 2 indicates that another psychologist thinks that this problem is the second most important, and so on.

To find the interquartile range, first put the ranks in order from low to high and then divide it into quarters as shown in Example 10.5.1. As you can see, there are four ranks below 2.5, four ranks between 2.5 and 6.5, four ranks between 6.5 and 9.5, and four ranks above 9.5. Thus, the middle 50% lies between 2.5 and 9.5. What is the value of the interquartile range? It is calculated as follows: 9.5 − .25 = 7.0. Thus, we can report that the interquartile range is 7.0, which means that the middle 50% of the respondents lie within 7 rank order points of each other.

Example 10.5.1 *Ranks divided into quarters*

1, 1, 1, 2, 3, 4, 5, 6, 7, 8, 8, 9, 10, 11, 11, 12
　　　⇧　　　　⇧　　　　⇧
　　　2.5　　　6.5　　　9.5

---

[5] The term *outlier* is a statistical term that refers to a small number of scores that are very distant from the other scores in a distribution. If there are outliers at one end of a distribution but not the other end, they create a skewed distribution.

Guideline 10.6   If the mean has been selected as the average, use the standard deviation as the measure of variability.

Often a distribution of scores is described with only two statistics: the *mean* to describe its average, and the *standard deviation* to describe its variability. The mean was recommended earlier in this chapter for describing the average of interval data that are *not* highly skewed.

Remember that the term *variability* refers to the extent to which respondents vary or differ from each other. Let's see what this means by considering the three groups in Example 10.6.1, all of which have the same mean but different standard deviations on an attitude scale. Note that the symbol for the standard deviation is S or SD.[6]

Example 10.6.1   *Means and standard deviations for three groups of scores*

Attitude scores for Group A: 15, 15, 15, 15, 15, 15, 15
$$M = 15.00, S = 0.00$$

Attitude scores for Group B: 14, 14, 14, 15, 16, 16, 16
$$M = 15.00, S = 0.93$$

Attitude scores for Group C: 0, 5, 10, 15, 20, 25, 30
$$M = 15.00, S = 10.00$$

As you can see in Example 10.6.1, all three groups have the same average (that is, the same mean as indicated by M), yet they are different in their variability. Group A has no variability among its scores, which is indicated by its standard deviation of 0.00. Group B has a little more variability among its scores than Group A, as indicated by its standard deviation of .93. Group C has much more variability than either Group A or Group B. (Notice there are large differences among Group C's scores.) The much larger variability among Group C's scores is indicated by its standard deviation of 10.00. Example 10.6.1 clearly indicates that the larger the differences among the scores, the larger the standard deviation will be.

What makes a standard deviation large or small? The answer is how far the scores are from the mean of the group. When all the scores are the same as the mean, such as Group A's scores in Example 10.6.1, the standard deviation is zero. When the scores differ greatly from their mean, which is the case for Group C (for example, scores such as 0, 5, 25, and 30 are far from the mean of 15.00), the standard deviation will be large.

---

[6] Technically, the upper-case S or SD indicates that the standard deviation is based on a study of a population, while the lower-case s or sd indicates that the standard deviation is based on a sample. It is a good idea to follow this convention when writing research reports, but many applied researchers ignore it.

We will consider how to compute the standard deviation using Group C's scores. First, list the scores in the first column of a table, as shown in Example 10.6.2. Second, subtract the mean (15.00) from each score, yielding the *difference scores*. Third, square each difference score as shown in the last column of the table. Fourth, sum the scores as shown in the last column. After constructing a table such as the one in Example 10.6.2, simply enter the values as shown in the formula below.

Example 10.6.2

Table 10.6.2   *Worktable for computing the standard deviation*

A score	minus	the mean	equals	the difference.	Then, square the difference.
0	–	15	=	−15	225
5	–	15	=	−10	100
10	–	15	=	−5	25
15	–	15	=	0	0
20	–	15	=	5	25
25	–	15	=	10	100
30	–	15	=	15	225
					Total = 700

To get the standard deviation, use this formula, in which the *total* is the sum of the last column in Table 10.6.2 (in this case, 700), and N is the number of cases (in this case, 7 since there are 7 scores):

$$S = \sqrt{\frac{total}{N}} = \sqrt{\frac{700}{7}} = \sqrt{100} = 10.0$$

It turns out that the formula you just learned is for use when you have studied an entire population. To get the standard deviation when you have studied a sample, use this slightly modified formula:[7]

$$s = \sqrt{\frac{total}{n-1}}$$

Of course, you will want to use a computer to perform the calculations when you have a large number of scores.

---

[7] The only difference is subtracting the constant 1 in the denominator. You may recall that we are using upper-case letters for statistics based on populations and lower-case letters for statistics based on samples.

Guideline 10.7   Keep in mind that the standard deviation has a special relationship to the normal curve that helps in its interpretation.

The normal curve is a bell-shaped distribution that is found very widely in nature. For example, the heights of women (or men) in large populations are distributed normally, the weights of diamonds found in nature are distributed normally, and the length of monkeys' arms are distributed normally.

Example 10.7.1 shows the characteristic shape of a normal curve. It indicates, for example, that most women are near the average in height (which is why the curve is high in the middle). Also, there is variability on both sides of the average, and the curve falls off evenly on both sides, creating a tail to the left (small numbers of very short women) and a tail to the right (small numbers of very tall women).

Example 10.7.1

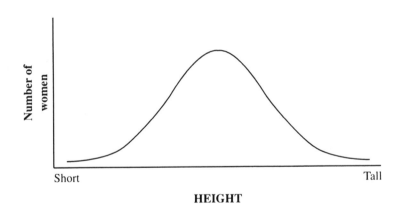

Figure 10.7.1   *The normal curve*

Researchers conducting questionnaire research often find that respondents' scores are approximately normally distributed. When this is the case, keep in mind that the standard deviation has a special relationship to the normal curve: *68% of the respondents lies within one standard deviation unit of the mean* (that is, the mean plus/minus the standard deviation). For example, if you read in a report that $M = 70$ and $S = 10$ for a normal distribution of responses, you would know that 68% of the respondents have scores between 60 (that is, the mean of 70 minus the standard deviation of 10) and 80 (that is, the mean of 70 plus the standard deviation of 10). This is illustrated in Example 10.7.2.

Example 10.7.2

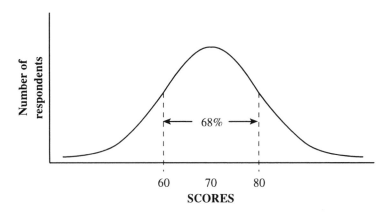

Figure 10.7.2   *The normal curve with a mean of 70 and a standard deviation of 10*

Keep in mind that there are only two rules for selecting a measure of variability:
1. Use the interquartile range if the median has been selected as the average.
2. Use the standard deviation if the mean has been selected as the average.

Exercise for Chapter 10

1. If you ask respondents to rank order a list of traits of effective administrators, you are collecting what type of data? (Circle one.)
   A. ordinal   B. equal interval

2. According to this chapter, data collected with Likert-type items are usually considered to represent what type of data? (Circle one.)
   A. ordinal   B. equal interval

3. Which average is recommended for use with ordinal data?

4. Which average is recommended for use with highly skewed equal interval data?

5. Which average is recommended for use with equal interval data that are not highly skewed?

6. What is the mean of the following set of scores?

9, 7, 3, 10, 2

7. What is the median of the scores in question 6?

8. On a questionnaire, children were asked to report how much money (to the nearest dollar) they put into the collection plate the last time they attended a religious service. The following distribution was obtained. Is it skewed? Explain. Which average should be computed to represent the average donation?

Table for question 8

Amount of donation to the nearest dollar	Frequency of response ($n = 80$)
$50.00	1
$25.00	1
$20.00	2
$5.00	10
$4.00	11
$3.00	12
$2.00	18
$1.00	25

9. Which of the following measures of variability should be used very sparingly? (Circle one.)
   A. range   B. interquartile range   C. standard deviation

10. If the mean has been selected as the average for a distribution, which measure of variability should be used? (Circle one.)
   A. range   B. interquartile range   C. standard deviation

11. According to the following table, which group has the more variability in their scores? Explain.

Table for question 11

	M	S
Group A	10.32	2.98
Group B	12.77	2.05

12. According to the table for question 11, which group has the higher average score? Explain.

Chapter 11

Describing Relationships

In this chapter, we will consider basic statistical methods for examining relationships between two variables. For example, we might want to know whether there is a relationship between gender and political affiliation or a relationship between attitudes toward reading and attitudes toward school.

Guideline 11.1   For the relationship between two nominal variables, prepare a contingency table.

Nominal data was defined under Guideline 9.3 in Chapter 9 as naming data — data generated by respondents who name with words the categories to which they belong. For example, if respondents name their gender or name the country they were born in, they are producing nominal data.

A *contingency table* is a two-way table that simultaneously shows the two categories to which each respondent belongs. To see what this means, consider Example 11.1.1 in which there is only one respondent, which is indicated by the face (☺). The table simultaneously provides information on two variables (characteristics of the respondent): (1) she attended the stop-smoking program, and (2) she is not smoking currently.

Example 11.1.1

Table 11.1.1 *Contingency table with one respondent*

		Attended the stop-smoking program?	
		Yes	No
Smoking currently?	Yes		
	No	☺	

Let's suppose we administered a questionnaire on smoking to a group and obtained the frequencies in Example 11.1.2. (To get the frequencies, simply tally the number who attended the workshop and are smoking currently, then tally the number who did not attend the workshop and are smoking currently, and so on.)

105

Example 11.1.2

Table 11.1.2   *Contingency table with frequencies for a group of respondents*

		Attended the stop-smoking program?	
		Yes	No
Smoking currently?	Yes	0	50
	No	50	0
	Total	50	50

The frequencies in the contingency table in Example 11.1.2 show a perfect relationship: If we know that a person attended the stop-smoking program, we can predict with perfect accuracy (at least for the 100 respondents represented in the table) that they are not smoking currently. Of course, this example is for instructional purposes only so you can see an example of a perfect relationship, which serves as a reference point when interpreting other relationships. Unfortunately, real stop-smoking programs are far from perfectly effective, and it is exceedingly rare to find perfect relationships when studying people.

Example 11.1.3 illustrates a more realistic example, in which there is a less than perfect relationship. However, it still indicates that there is a relationship: Those who use the Internet more frequently are more opposed to censorship of sexual material on the Internet than those who use it less frequently.

Example 11.1.3

Table 11.1.3   *Contingency table with frequencies for a group of respondents*

		Frequency of Internet use		
		Frequent	Occasional	Seldom
Favors censorship of sexual material on the Internet?	Yes	30	43	55
	No	60	47	35
	Total	90	90	90

Guideline 11.2   When groups have unequal numbers of respondents, include percentages in contingency tables.

Often, you will obtain unequal numbers of respondents in comparison groups. When this is the case, comparison of frequencies in contingency tables can be confusing. Consider Example 11.2.1, where there is a sample of 29 respondents who had been on welfare and 148 who had never been on welfare. Is there a relationship between having been on welfare and being in favor of government funding of welfare? The relationship is easier to see if we consider the percentages presented in Example 11.2.2, where it is clear that a majority of those who had been on welfare favor it while a majority of those who had not been on welfare oppose it. (Note that the percentages were calculated separately for each column. For example, for the first data cell in the first column of Table 11.2.1, which has a frequency of 19, the percentage was obtained by dividing 19 by the total for the column, 29, and multiplying the result by 100.)

Example 11.2.1

Table 11.2.1 *Contingency table with frequencies for a group of respondents*

		Ever received welfare?	
		Yes	No
In favor of	Yes	19	67
welfare?	No	10	81
	Total	29	148

Example 11.2.2

Table 11.2.2 *Contingency table with frequencies and percentages for a group of respondents*

		Ever received welfare?	
		Yes	No
In favor of	Yes	66% (n = 19)	45% (n = 67)
welfare?	No	34% (n = 10)	55% (n = 81)
	Total	100% (n = 29)	100% (n = 148)

Guideline 11.3   For the relationship between two equal interval variables, compute a correlation coefficient.

Equal interval data was defined under Guideline 10.2 in Chapter 10. Responses to Likert-type items (i.e., items with "Strongly agree" to "Strongly disagree" choices) and total scores on attitude scales are widely assumed to be equal interval. In addition, some demographic variables are measured on equal interval scales. Years of education completed is an example; it is equal interval because the difference between 1 year and 2 years is equal to the difference between 2 years and 3 years, and so on.

The most widely used statistic for describing the relationship between two equal interval variables is the *Pearson product-moment correlation coefficient,* which is often simply called the *Pearson r*. (Note that *r* is the symbol selected by Karl Pearson, the statistician who developed the correlation coefficient.)

Consider Example 11.3.1, which shows the scores on an attitude toward technology scale and the scores on an attitude toward the Internet scale. The attitude toward technology scale had many more items than the one on the Internet, so the scores tend to be much higher on the former. However, for our purpose here, we are not interested in this artifact produced by the different numbers of items. Instead, we are interested in the relationship between the two variables. We can determine whether there is a relationship by considering positions of the individuals on the two variables relative to others in the group. This is easier than it sounds. For example, Joe and Jane have high scores on attitudes toward technology. (Notice that their scores of 35 and 32 are higher than the scores obtained by others on this scale.) Likewise, Joe and Jane have high scores on attitudes toward the Internet. (Notice that their scores of 9 and 10 are higher than the scores obtained by others on this scale.) At the same time, those who have low attitudes toward technology scores (John and Jake) also have low scores on attitudes toward the Internet. This illustrates what we mean by a *direct relationship* (also called a *positive relationship*). In a direct relationship, high scores are associated with high scores, *and* low scores are associated with low scores.

Example 11.3.1

Table 11.3.1   *A direct relationship, r = .89*

Respondent	Attitude toward technology	Attitude toward the Internet
Joe	35	9
Jane	32	10
Marilyn	29	8
Phyllis	27	8
Homer	25	7
Clyde	22	8
Jennifer	21	6
Jake	18	4
John	15	5

Notice that the relationship in Example 11.3.1 is not perfect. For example, although Joe has a higher technology attitude than Jane, Jane has a higher Internet attitude than Joe. (In other words, while the order on the two variables is similar, it is not exactly the same; hence, the relationship is less than perfect.) If the relationship were perfect, the value of the Pearson *r* would be 1.00. Being less than perfect, its actual value is .89. As you can see in the following figure, which shows the possible values of the Pearson *r*, .89 is a strong direct relationship.

−1.00		Inverse Relationship		0.00		Direct Relationship		+1.00
⇧	⇧	⇧	⇧	⇧	⇧	⇧	⇧	⇧
perfect	strong	moderate	weak	none	weak	moderate	strong	perfect

In an *inverse relationship* (also called a *negative relationship*), those who are high on one variable are low on the other. Such a relationship exists between the two variables in Example 11.3.2. Those who are high in their fear of animals (such as Robert, Sheldon, and Cynthia) are low in age, while those who are low in their fear of animals are high in age. However, the relationship is not perfect. The value of the Pearson r for the relationship in the example is −.85.

Example 11.3.2

Table 11.3.2   *An inverse relationship, r = −.85*

Respondent	Fear of animals score	Age in years
Robert	10	9
Sheldon	8	8
Cynthia	9	7
Nancy	7	12
Elaine	7	13
Turner	6	15
Jackie	4	15
Tom	1	16
Sheila	0	16

The relationships in Examples 11.3.1 and 11.3.2 are strong, but in each case, there are exceptions, which make the Pearson rs less than 1.00 and −1.00. As the number and size of the exceptions increase, the values of the Pearson r become closer to 0.00. In fact, a value of 0.00 indicates a complete absence of a relationship. That is, when r equals 0.00, there is no discernable trend for the scores on the two variables to put respondents in the same or reverse orders.

For those of you who wish to try your hand at calculating a Pearson r using a calculator, the formula and an example are given in Appendix A.

Guideline 11.4   Interpret a Pearson *r* using the coefficient of determination.

It is important to note that the Pearson r is not a proportion and *cannot* be multiplied by 100 to get a percentage. For instance, a Pearson r of .50 does not correspond to 50% of anything. To think about correlation in terms of percentages, we must convert Pearson rs to another statistic, the *coefficient of determination*, whose symbol is r^2, which indicates how to compute it—simply square r. Thus, for an r of .50, r^2 equals .25 (.50 x .50 = .25). If we multiply .25 by 100, we get 25%. What does this result mean? Simply this: A Pearson r of .50 is 25% better than 0.00. Example 11.4.1 shows selected values of r, r^2, and the percentages you should think about when interpreting an r.

Example 11.4.1

Table 11.4.1   *Selected values of r and r²*

r	r^2	Percentage better than zero[*]
.90	.81	81%
.50	.25	25%
.25	.06	6%
−.25	.06	6%
−.50	.25	25%
−.90	.81	81%

[*]Also called *percentage of variance accounted for* or *percentage of explained variance.*

Note that it is conventional to give the values of Pearson rs in a research report. However, while discussing the values, it is helpful to consider how much better than 0.00 they are. For example, a naïve researcher might describe a Pearson r of .25 as indicating a moderate correlation. In light of the fact that .25 is only 6% greater than zero, a better interpretation would be that it indicates a weak or relatively weak relationship.

Guideline 11.5   For the relationship between a nominal variable and an equal interval variable, examine differences among averages.

In Example 11.5.1, the nominal variable is political affiliation (Democrat and Republican). The equal interval variable is attitudes toward abortion measured with an attitude scale that has a possible score range from 0 to 100, where 100 indicates the most favorable attitude. By comparing the means[1] for the different categories on the nominal variable, we can see that there is a relationship between the two variables such that Democrats have more favorable attitudes toward abortion than Republicans. In other words, these results indicate that a respondent's political affiliation is predictive of his or her attitude toward abortion.

---

[1] You should recall from Chapter 10 that the *mean* is the average we use with equal interval data that are not highly skewed. For highly skewed equal interval data and for ordinal data, compare *medians* instead of means.

Example 11.5.1

Table 11.5.1   *Attitudes toward abortion*

	M	SD
Democrat	55.68	9.86
Republican	42.71	7.99

The standard deviations help in the interpretation of the relationship in Table 11.5.1. (See Guidelines 10.6 and 10.7 in Chapter 10 to review the standard deviation.) These standard deviations indicate that there is considerable variation among those with both political affiliations. For example, assuming that the distribution of attitude scores is normal, the standard deviation of 9.86 for Democrats indicates that you need to go out almost 10 points on each side of their mean to gather 68% of the Democrats, and the remaining 32% of the Democrats are even farther than 10 points from their mean. Put another way, neither the Democrats nor the Republicans are very homogenous in their attitudes toward abortion. Thus, a respondent's political affiliation is a far-from-perfect predictor of his or her attitudes.

Concluding Comment

While we have only started to scratch the surface of the various techniques that statisticians have developed for examining relationships, those described in this chapter will take you a long way toward getting started in considering the relationships among variables you measure with your questionnaires.

Those of you who have been closely following the chapters on statistics may have noticed that how to analyze *ordinal data* for relationships is not discussed in this chapter. (You may recall that you were advised to avoid collecting ordinal data by Guideline 2.13.) As it turns out, you may substitute the term *ordinal* for *equal interval* throughout this chapter and follow the information in the guidelines for analyzing data—keeping in mind that the median, and not the mean, should be used as an average for ordinal data.[2]

---

[2] For the relationship between two ordinal variables, many researchers use the Spearman rank-order correlation coefficient. As it turns out, the value you will get using Spearman's method is the same (except for differences due to rounding) as you will get using the formula for the Pearson *r*. The Spearman method is somewhat easier to use than the Pearson method if you are calculating a correlation coefficient using a calculator rather than a computer. For most practical purposes, the two methods are the same.

Exercise for Chapter 11

1. What is the name of the type of table you should build in order to examine the relationship between two nominal variables?

2. Fill in the blanks in the contingency table presented below for this data:

Respondent	High school graduate?	Employed currently?
James	Yes	Yes
Rudolph	No	No
Stacey	No	Yes
Lucy	No	No
Randall	No	Yes
Fernando	Yes	Yes
Mary	No	Yes
Jessica	Yes	Yes
Hubert	No	No
Casey	No	No

Contingency table for question 2

		High school graduate? Yes	High school graduate? No
Employed currently?	Yes	___% (*n* = ___)	___% (*n* = ___)
	No	___% (*n* = ___)	___% (*n* = ___)
	Total	___% (*n* = ___)	___% (*n* = ___)

3. Describe in words the relationship revealed by the contingency table for question 2.

4. Suppose you found a Pearson *r* of .85 for the relationship between attitudes toward physicians and attitudes toward registered nurses. This relationship is best described as
   A. strong.   B. moderate.   C. weak.

5. What is the value of the Pearson r when there is no relationship whatsoever between two variables?

6. A Pearson r should be used to describe the relationship between which two types of variables?
   A. two nominal variables   B. two equal interval variables

7. Fill in the blanks in the following table by computing the means for those who are divorced and those who are not divorced. Compute the means to three decimal places and round to two places. Attitude toward divorce was measured with a scale on which higher scores indicate more favorable attitudes toward divorce.

Respondent	Divorced?	Attitude Toward Divorce Score
Martha	No	24
Madeline	No	33
Maryanne	Yes	42
Melissa	No	40
Melody	Yes	50
Maria	Yes	49
Mary	Yes	45
Michelle	No	30
Misty	No	35

Table for question 7

	M
Divorced	____
Not divorced	____

8. Describe in words the relationship revealed by the table you constructed for question 7.

9. In question 7, which variable is nominal, and which one is equal interval?

Notes:

Chapter 12

Estimating Margins of Error

You may recall from Chapter 8 that a population is any group of interest to a researcher. It may be small, such as all seniors in a high school, or it may be large, such as all adults residing in a state. When a population is fairly small, we often conduct a *census*, which is a study of all members of a population. When studying large populations, we usually administer a questionnaire to just a sample and infer that what we learn about the sample is also true of the population.

You may also recall from Chapter 8 that *random sampling*, which gives every member of a population an equal chance of being selected, is highly recommended, but it creates *sampling errors* (that is, *chance errors due to random sampling*). In this chapter, we will consider some ways to evaluate sampling errors.

Guideline 12.1   It is extremely difficult, and often impossible, to evaluate the effects of a bias in sampling.

A sample is biased when some individuals or subgroups in a population have a greater chance of being included in a sample than others do. For example, you will obtain biased samples (1) if you administer a questionnaire only to volunteers from a professional association when you are interested in the responses of all members of the association or (2) if you administer a questionnaire only to your neighbors when you are interested in the attitudes of all voters in your city. Each particular bias has its own unique characteristics. For instance, the bias created by surveying my neighbors will undoubtedly be different in magnitude and perhaps in direction than the bias created by surveying your neighbors. The uniqueness of each bias makes it nearly impossible to get a good statistical estimate of its effects on the results. (Put another way, there are no statistical tools developed specifically for evaluating the effects of a bias created by surveying only your neighbors.)

In contrast, we can evaluate the possible effects of sampling errors because they are random errors, and random errors *in the long run* always have the same characteristics. While it is beyond the scope of this book to delve into the theory underlying this premise, you can get a handle on it if you consider tossing a coin. If I toss it 10 times, I could easily get 7 heads and 3 tails instead of 5 heads and 5 tails *quite at random*. If you also toss it 10 times, you could easily get 3 heads and 7 tails. However, the laws that govern random events tell us that if we each toss it enough times — perhaps 2,000 times — we should each get very close to (if not exactly) an even split (1,000-1,000).[1] Thus, in the long run, we know how random errors operate. This knowledge is the basis for the remaining guidelines in this chapter.

Guideline 12.2   When evaluating a percentage, consider the standard error of a percentage.

The *standard error of a percentage* is what is popularly known as the *margin of error for a percentage*. Margins of error are widely reported for results of political polls reported in the mass media. For example, if you read that 55% approve of the president's handling of the economy and are told to allow +/– 4%, you can be rather confident that the true percentage that approves is between 51% (55% minus 4%) and 59% (55% plus 4%). Note that we need a margin of error because only a sample was questioned, and the sample result may be off by as much as 4%.

It is very easy to compute a margin of error for a percentage. The formula is shown in Example 12.2.1.[2]

Example 12.2.1

In response to a questionnaire item, 75% of a simple random sample of 100 teachers in a school district reported that they feel very competent using the Internet to obtain information. To calculate the margin of error, the following formula was used, where P is the percentage who reported feeling competent (that is, 75), Q is 100 minus P (that is, $100 - 75 = 25$), and n is the number of respondents (that is, 100).

$$S_P = \sqrt{\frac{PQ}{n}} = \sqrt{\frac{(75)(25)}{100}} = \sqrt{\frac{1,875}{100}} = \sqrt{18.75} = 4.33$$

For reasons that are beyond the scope of this book, the standard error of a percentage when calculated as shown in Example 12.2.1 is a *68% margin of error*. That is, although 75% of the sample said they felt very competent using the Internet, we can be only 68% confident that the *true percentage in the whole population* that feels very competent lies within 4.33 percentage points of 75%.

It turns out that we can manipulate the 68% margin of error to get a margin with any degree of confidence that we wish to have. The most common is the *95% margin of error*. This is easy to obtain: Simply multiply the 68% margin of error

---

[1] If we don't get close to a 1,000-1,000 split, we may have a biased coin, such as a coin that is a bit heavier on one side than the other.

[2] In this chapter, we will be considering margins of error for *simple random sampling*. The margins may be slightly different if other sampling methods are used such as *stratified random sampling*. The method presented here is accurate only for samples of 60 or more respondents.

by 1.96. Thus, for our example, the 95% margin of error equals 4.33 x 1.96 = 8.48. (Note that the 1.96 is a constant; use it for all problems of this type regardless of the values of your specific results.) The 95% margin of error for our example means that we can be 95% confident that the true percentage of teachers in the population who feel competent using the Internet is between 66.52% (75% − 8.48% = 66.52%) and 83.48% (75% + 8.48% = 83.48%).

Based on the sample of 100 in Example 12.2.1, our best estimate is that the percentage who feel competent is 75%, but we have to allow more than 8 percentage points (specifically, 8.48 points for 95% confidence) on each side of this estimate for the possible effects of random errors produced by random sampling. With a margin of error of more than 8 percentage points, our result is not very precise. How can we get more precise results? By using a larger sample. This is illustrated in Example 12.2.2 where another researcher used a sample of 1,000. As you can see, with a sample of 1,000, the 68% margin of error is only 1.37 points (instead of 4.33 when a sample of 100 was used), and the more commonly used 95% margin of error is only 2.69 points (instead of 8.48 when a sample of 100 was used).

Example 12.2.2

A researcher conducted the same study as the one in Example 12.2.1 and obtained the same result: 75% of the sample indicated that they feel very competent using the Internet to obtain information. However, this researcher used a sample of 1,000 respondents and thus obtained much smaller margins of error than the first researcher. Here are the calculations for the second researcher:

$$S_P = \sqrt{\frac{PQ}{n}} = \sqrt{\frac{(75)(25)}{1,000}} = \sqrt{\frac{1,875}{1,000}} = \sqrt{1.87} = 1.37$$

Thus, the 68% margin of error is only 1.37 points. For the 95% margin of error, multiply this result by 1.96, which yields 2.7.

The researcher who conducted the study in Example 12.2.2 can now report that the percentage of teachers who feel very competent using the Internet is 75% with a margin of error of 2.7 points. (Remember that we usually report the 95% margin of error—not the 68% margin. Thus, we are reporting 2.7 as the value of the margin of error.) In reports in the mass media, the degree of confidence is often not indicated. For more statistically sophisticated audiences than the general public, it is a good idea to state that the reader should allow 2.7 points for 95% confidence.

Guideline 12.3   When evaluating a mean, consider the standard error of the mean.

You should recall from Chapter 10 that the mean is the average that is used to describe equal interval data that are not highly skewed. If you draw a random sample from a population and compute its mean as an estimate of the population mean, your estimate may be in error because of random sampling errors. The margin of error for a mean (that is, the standard error of the mean) is easy to compute as illustrated in Example 12.3.1

Example 12.3.1

A random sample of 90 hospital social workers was surveyed with a questionnaire. Among other things, the questionnaire measured their attitudes toward patients with HIV/AIDS with a set of items that could yield scores from 0 to 100 (with higher scores indicating more favorable attitudes). Their mean attitude score for the sample was 72.5, and the standard deviation was 10.3. To calculate the margin of error, the following formula was used, where s is the standard deviation (that is, 10.3) and n is the number of respondents (that is, 90).

$$S_m = \frac{s}{\sqrt{n}} = \frac{10.3}{\sqrt{90}} = \frac{10.3}{9.49} = 1.09$$

The standard error of the mean as calculated in Example 12.3.1 is a *68% margin of error*. Just as with the standard error of a percentage that we examined earlier, we multiply it by 1.96 to get the *95% margin of error*. Thus, 1.09 x 1.96 = 2.1. This means that we can be 95% confident that the mean for the population lies within 2.1 points of the sample mean of 72.5.

The researcher who conducted the study in Example 12.3.1 can now report that the mean attitude score is 72.5, the standard deviation is 10.3, and the margin of error for the mean is 2.1 points. For statistically sophisticated audiences, the fact that the margin of error is for 95% confidence should be indicated.

Note that the procedure for getting the 95% margin of error for a mean is accurate only when using samples of about 60 or more respondents. For smaller samples, an adjustment should be made in the computations, which is shown in Appendix A.

Guideline 12.4   When evaluating a median, consider the standard error of the median.

You should recall from Chapter 10 that the median is the average we use for ordinal data and for equal interval data that are highly skewed. The computation of the standard error of the median is almost the same as for the mean —with the addition of a constant (1.253) as a multiplier in the numerator. This is the formula:

$$S_{median} = \frac{1.253s}{\sqrt{n}}$$

The use and interpretation of the standard error of the median is the same as that for the standard error of the mean. However, note that for the same set of data, the standard error of the median will be larger than the standard error of the mean. This results from the multiplier of 1.253 in the numerator, which increases the value of the numerator (remember that as the numerator of a fraction gets larger, the total fraction gets larger — for example, 2/3 is larger than 1/3). This is one reason why the mean is preferred to the median whenever the data permit its use.

Guideline 12.5   Consider building confidence intervals, especially when comparing two or more groups.

Up to this point in this chapter, you learned how to compute and interpret standard errors for a percentage, a mean, and a median. Example 12.5.1 shows how you might report such information. Remember that standard errors are often called *margins of error* in informal reports.

Example 12.5.1

The mean of the sample equals 72.5, and the standard deviation equals 10.3. The 95% margin of error for the mean equals 2.1 points.

To interpret the statistics in Example 12.5.1, consumers of your research must think about the mean of 72.5 plus/minus the margin of error of 2.1 points. As a courtesy to your consumers, you could perform the calculations for them and report what is known as a *confidence interval* instead of reporting the margin of error. Calculating the confidence interval is easy: (1) subtract the margin of error from the mean (72.5 – 2.1 = 70.4) and then (2) add the margin of error to the mean (72.5 + 2.1 = 74.6). Example 12.5.2 shows how this might be reported.

Example 12.5.2

The mean of the sample equals 72.5, and the standard deviation equals 10.3. The 95% confidence interval for the mean is 70.4 –74.6.

For consumers who are not familiar with confidence intervals, you could add this sentence:
Thus, we can be 95% confident that the population mean lies between 70.4 and 74.6.

Confidence intervals are especially helpful when comparing groups to establish differences among them. Let's suppose that the researcher who reported the results in Example 12.5.2 based on a sample of hospital social workers (who got a mean of 72.5) also surveyed a sample of licensed vocational nurses employed by the same hospitals with the same attitude scale and obtained a mean of 62.5. Sure, there's a 10-point difference between the two means, but since each mean may be in error because of random sampling, it's a good idea to compare the two confidence intervals, which are shown in Example 12.5.3.

Example 12.5.3

Table 12.5.3 *Statistics for two groups on attitudes toward patients with HIV/AIDS*

Group	Mean	Standard Deviation	95% Confidence Interval
Social Workers ($n = 90$)	72.5	10.3	70.4–74.5
Vocational Nurses ($n = 120$)	62.5	11.9	60.4–64.6

Notice in Example 12.5.3 that not only do the two means indicate that the two groups are different, but the two confidence intervals confirm that there probably is a difference because they *do not overlap*. Look at it this way: We have 95% confidence that the population mean for the social workers is somewhere between 70.4 and 74.5, and none of these possible values for the social workers' mean includes any of the possible values for the vocational nurses' mean (60.4 to 64.6). Thus, we can have considerable confidence that the two groups are, in truth, different (that is, it's unlikely that random errors alone are responsible for the difference). Put another way, even when we take account of random errors with confidence intervals, the difference seems to be reliable.

Since the information we obtain by considering whether confidence intervals overlap is very important, let's consider another example. This time, we'll use percentages. (The method for getting a 95% confidence interval for a percentage is the same as for the mean: Multiply the standard error of the percentage by 1.96; then add the result to the percentage and subtract it from the percentage.) Example 12.5.4 shows the percentages of teachers in Districts A and B who reported feeling competent using the Internet to obtain information. In this example, the two confidence intervals *overlap*. (Note that the confidence interval estimate for District A is as low as 66.52, while the confidence interval estimate for District B is as high as 74.52. Thus, it is possible that a larger percentage of the population of District B feels competent than the percentage of the population of District A that feels competent.) Because they overlap, we need to conclude that the difference is *not* reliable at the 95% confidence level. From a statistical point of view, the two samples of teachers are the same.

Example 12.5.4

Table 12.5.4 *Statistics for two groups on competence in using the Internet*

Group	Percentage who feel competent	95% confidence interval
Teachers in District A ($n = 100$)	75%	66.52–83.48
Teachers in District B ($n = 80$)	64%	53.48–74.52

Remember:
- When the two confidence intervals do *not* overlap, the difference should be described as reliable.
- When the two confidence intervals overlap, the difference should be described as unreliable.

Comparing confidence intervals to see if they overlap is an informal way of checking for statistical significance. A brief introduction to formal significance testing is presented in Appendix B.

Exercise for Chapter 12

1. Margins of error take into account (circle one)
   A. bias in sampling.   B. random sampling errors.   C. both A and B.

2. A random sample of 200 recent graduates from a program was surveyed with a questionnaire. Sixty percent of them reported that they had found full-time employment in the field of psychology. To two decimal places, what is the 68% margin of error for this result?

3. For question 2, what is the 95% margin of error?

4. What is the 95% confidence interval for question 2?

5. A random sample of 40 high school seniors was administered a questionnaire that measured their attitude toward safe-sex practices. On a scale from 0 to 100, their mean was 83.4 and their standard deviation was 12.9. To two decimal places, what is the 68% margin of error for their mean?

6. For question 5, what is the 95% margin of error?

7. What is the 95% confidence interval for question 5?

8. Researchers administered a questionnaire to *all* physical education teachers in a school district (their population of interest). Would it be appropriate for them to consider margins of error when interpreting their results? Why? Why not?

9. Consider the statistics based on two samples in the following table. Do the two confidence intervals overlap?

Table for question 9: Statistics for two samples of high school graduates

Group	Percentage accepted to college	95% confidence interval
Graduates of Smith High School ($n = 300$)	42%	36.41–47.59
Graduates of Doe High School ($n = 280$)	34%	28.45–39.55

10. Should the difference between the two percentages in question 9 be described as reliable? Explain.

Chapter 13

Writing Reports of Questionnaire Research

In this chapter, we will consider some basic guidelines for writing two types of research reports: (1) informal, newspaper-like reports and (2) formal, academic reports. If you are writing some other type such as a business research report for your employer, consider all the guidelines in this chapter and follow those that you think will best meet the needs of the readers of your report.

If you are using this book as a guide for conducting a class project in a research methods class, ask your instructor what type of report you should write.

Guideline 13.1   In an informal report, variations in the organization of the report are permitted.

An informal report in a college newspaper might begin with, "More than 60% of the students on this campus favor continuing affirmative action in admissions policies." This could be followed by other details of the results such as, "Women are more in favor than men by a margin of 3 to 2."

If space permits, consider including some or all of the questions in your questionnaire. Readers often like to see how they would respond to the actual questions. This should be followed by a brief description of your research methods — especially, how many students responded to the questionnaire and how the sample was selected.

If the topic of your research is especially timely, you might want to incorporate some information on its timeliness (for example, "The study was conducted five days after the college trustees voted to abolish affirmative action in admissions.").

Variations in the organization of informal reports are permitted. A general guideline is that the first sentence (or at least the first paragraph) should refer to the main topic of the research. For instance, if your research is on students' views on affirmative action in admissions, do not start an informal report with a history of affirmative action or a description of how the governor of the state appoints college trustees with approval of the state assembly.

Guideline 13.2   Academic reports should begin with a formal introduction that cites literature.

The introduction should state why the research problem is important and provide an overview of what has already been said about the topic in the literature.[1] Point out how your study differs from others that have already been reported. For example: "All of the studies cited here were conducted prior to the recent Supreme Court ruling on affirmative action" or "While the respondents in the previous studies were members of the general public, the respondents in this study were students attending Academia College." The introduction should end with a statement describing your specific research objectives or hypotheses.

Guideline 13.3   The second section of academic reports should describe the research methods.

Start this section with the main heading **Method**, which may be centered. Follow it with the subheadings *Respondents*, *The Questionnaire*, and *Procedure* as shown in Example 13.3.1.

Example 13.3.1 shows some of the things that might be discussed in the Method section. Note that it is essential to state under the subheading *Respondents* how the respondents were selected, how many responded, and how many failed to respond.[2] If demographic information has been collected, it should also be described here.[3]

Under the subheading *The Questionnaire*, it is essential to give an overview of how the questionnaire was developed, including a brief description of tryouts and item analyses, if any.[4] If the actual questionnaire will be included in the report, either as a figure or an appendix, the writer is obliged to describe it only very briefly. If it is not included, the writer should describe the questionnaire in more detail and, at an absolute minimum, should indicate how many items there were in each section of the questionnaire and their form (e.g., open-ended, Likert-type, and so on). It's a good idea to provide sample items if the whole questionnaire will not be included in the report.

Use the subsection on *Procedure* to provide details on when and how the questionnaires were distributed and collected or returned. Also, if informed consent was obtained, it is important to mention this fact.

---

[1] In theses and dissertations, it is traditional to provide the introduction in the first chapter and the literature review in the second chapter.

[2] The subheadings *Subjects* and *Participants* are often used in research reports instead of *Respondents*.

[3] Some researchers wait until the Results section to provide demographic information.

[4] Researchers often used the subtitle *Instrumentation* instead of *The Questionnaire*. *Instrumentation* refers to the measuring instruments such as a questionnaire.

Example 13.3.1

Method

Respondents

A simple random sample of 40 class sections was drawn from the master list of all 694 class sections at Academia College. The professors of 38 of the 40 class sections administered the questionnaire to their students during class time, which yielded a total of 652 respondents. Demographic questions on the questionnaire revealed that 72.9% of the respondents were undergraduates and 52% were…[and so on].

The Questionnaire

The questionnaire used in this research was developed by the author by following these steps.… A copy of the questionnaire is included in Appendix A.

Procedure

The 40 professors whose class sections were randomly selected were contacted by telephone by the researcher. The purpose of the research was described to them, and any questions they had about the research were answered. Two professors declined to have their students participate because their courses were field-work courses in which students did not meet as a group. Questionnaires were sent through the campus mail to the remaining 38 professors with a request that they administer them during the first week of November. All 38 professors returned the completed questionnaires through the campus mail by mid-November.

An informed consent form for this research was approved by Academia College's Human Rights Committee. Professors were asked to distribute the form to students prior to administering the questionnaire and to administer the questionnaire only to those students who consented to participate. All students in all classes signed the form acknowledging their informed consent.

Guideline 13.4   The third section of academic reports should describe the results.

This section should begin with the main heading **Results**, which may be centered. Some researchers prefer the main heading **Analysis and Results** when the method of analysis will be described in detail. Generally, however, it is not necessary to describe how commonly used statistics are computed.

Consider building statistical tables or figures to present your results. These are especially helpful when comparing groups. For example, Table 12.5.3 on page 120 makes it easy to compare social workers with vocational nurses. For each table, describe the main thrust of what it indicates and point out interesting details. For Table 12.5.3, you might state, "Table 12.5.3 indicates that, on average, social workers have a more positive attitude toward patients with HIV/AIDS than do vocational nurses. The fact that the confidence intervals for the means do not overlap indicates that this difference is reliable in light of sampling errors."

Sometimes it is possible to incorporate the actual wording from items in statistical tables. For an example, see Table 10.2.2 on page 96.

All tables and figures should be referred to in the text. A table or figure that is not worthy of mention in your narrative probably does not belong in your report.

Guideline 13.5   The last section of academic reports should be a discussion.

Use the main heading **Discussion** or **Discussion and Conclusions**, or **Summary and Discussion** to set off this section.

This section may begin with a summary of the previous sections in the report. This is especially helpful in long, complex reports since it keeps readers from getting lost in the details, and it sets the stage for your discussion.

In your discussion, describe the importance of your results and their implications. Implications indicate what a person or organization should do based on your results. Questionnaires used to evaluate products, services, and programs almost always have direct implications. For example, an implication of questionnaire research to evaluate a program might be that the program is highly effective and should be continued in its present form or that the program needs to be reformed in specific ways in light of weaknesses pointed out by respondents.

If your results differ from those previously reported in the literature, you may wish to speculate in your discussion on how they are different (for example, your questionnaire may have probed the issue in a different way with different items from those used by previous researchers). Keep in mind that you should *not* introduce new literature in your discussion. This is the section where you should be tying things together to reach a conclusion—not introducing new material. You may also wish to end with suggestions for others who might do research in this area in the future. If you do so, offer specific suggestions — not some general statement to the effect that more research is needed. An example of a specific suggestion is, "This research dealt only with students' attitudes on affirmative action in college admissions. In future research, it might be interesting to compare these attitudes with students' attitudes on affirmative action in employment to determine the pervasiveness of their attitudes."

Guideline 13.6   Acknowledge any weakness in your research methodology.

Weaknesses such as getting a low rate of return to a questionnaire or finding that some questionnaire items confused some respondents should be mentioned in your report. This shows the reader that you are knowledgeable enough to spot your own weaknesses and reminds your readers to use caution when considering your results. Some researchers prefer to acknowledge weakness in research methodology in the Method section of a report (for example, acknowledge that a low rate of return biases the results under the subheading *Respondents* in the Method section); others save a description of methodological weaknesses for the Discussion section.

Concluding Comment

Formal, academic reports are usually structured in the manner suggested by the above guidelines. However, exceptions can be made in the interests of presenting the material clearly. If you are writing with an eye to publishing in a particular journal, scan a number of articles in that journal to determine the typical organization. If you will be conducting questionnaire research for a thesis or dissertation, check with your committee on its expectations. Journal editors and committees often will recommend that you follow a particular style manual, which, among other things, describes the organization of research reports.[5]

Exercise for Chapter 13

Note: All questions in this exercise refer to formal, academic research reports.

1. "Reports should start with the results in order to get right to the heart of the matter." This statement is
   A. true.   B. false.

2. "The review of the literature should be appended at the end of the report." This statement is
   A. true.   B. false.

3. It is essential to provide what three types of information under the subheading *Respondents*?

---

[5] For more information on writing research reports, see Pyrczak, F. & Bruce, R. R. (2000). *Writing Empirical Research Reports: A Basic Guide for Students of the Social and Behavioral Sciences.* (3rd Ed.) Los Angeles: Pyrczak Publishing.

4. What are the three subheadings recommended for use under the main heading *Method*?

5. Demographic information on respondents usually should be presented in which section of a research report?

6. Is it appropriate for the *Results* section to contain only statistical tables and figures without a narrative description? Explain.

7. When is it especially helpful to begin the *Discussion* section with a summary?

8. Is it appropriate to end a research report with this simple statement: "More research is needed."? Explain.

9. Why should you acknowledge in your research report any weaknesses in your research methodology?

10. In which two parts of a research report do researchers typically acknowledge weaknesses in their research methodology?

Checklist of Guidelines

This checklist is designed to help you review the main points in this book. In addition, your instructor may wish to refer to the checklist numbers when commenting on your proposal for questionnaire research, your questionnaire items, and your research report.

Chapter 1: Planning Questionnaire Research

___ 1.1 Consider the advantages and disadvantages of using questionnaires.

___ 1.2 Prepare written objectives for the research.

___ 1.3 Have your objectives reviewed by others.

___ 1.4 Review the literature related to the objectives.

___ 1.5 Determine the feasibility of administering your questionnaire to the population of interest.

___ 1.6 Prepare a timeline.

Chapter 2: Writing Items to Collect Factual Information

___ 2.1 Consider asking respondents to recall behavior only over a limited, recent time period.

___ 2.2 Use "always" and "never" with caution.

___ 2.3 Avoid using negatives in statements.

___ 2.4 Each item should ask only a single question.

___ 2.5 Make the choices for an item exhaustive.

___ 2.6 Spell out acronyms and define difficult-to-understand terms.

___ 2.7 Underline, italicize, or use bold print to draw respondents' attention to important terms.

___ 2.8 Use "Don't know" sparingly as a choice.

___ 2.9 Be specific in your requests for information.

___ 2.10 Carefully consider using "Yes" and "No" as choices.

___ 2.11 Avoid putting a blank in the middle of an item.

___ 2.12 Make the choices mutually exclusive when only one choice is to be selected.

___ 2.13 Use items that require ranking sparingly.

___ 2.14 Use open-ended questions sparingly.

Chapter 3: Writing Items to Collect Demographic Information

___ 3.1 Ask about demographics sparingly.

___ 3.2 Avoid invading the privacy of "others" with demographic items.

___ 3.3 Consider providing ranges of values instead of asking for a precise value.

___ 3.4 Carefully consider the ranges of values you present in an item.

___ 3.5 Use care when writing questions about race or ethnicity.

___ 3.6 Use standard categories whenever possible.

___ 3.7 Consider placing demographic questions at the end of the questionnaire.

___ 3.8 Group together demographic questions and write a brief, separate introduction to them.

Chapter 4: Writing Items to Measure Attitudes

___ 4.1 Examine attitude scales that have already been developed.

___ 4.2 Consider using Likert-type items.

___ 4.3 The statement in a Likert-type item should deal with only one point.

___ 4.4 Consider whether to use "Neutral" or "Undecided" in Likert-type items.

___ 4.5 Use "Don't know" sparingly in Likert-type items.

___ 4.6 Use multiple items in an attitude scale.

___ 4.7 Prepare a list of the broad components of an attitude, and use it as the basis for writing an attitude scale.

___ 4.8 In an attitude scale, make some statements favorable and others unfavorable.

___ 4.9 Consider asking about reactions to hypothetical situations when necessary.

___ 4.10 Only use items that are clearly indicative of a favorable or unfavorable attitude.

___ 4.11 Label each point in a Likert-type item.

___ 4.12 Consider using a double-column format to present Likert-type items.

___ 4.13 Use simplified choices for children.

Chapter 5: Writing Items to Evaluate Products, Services, and Programs

___ 5.1 Name specific characteristics to be evaluated.

___ 5.2 Consider including an item to solicit an overall evaluation.

___ 5.3 Consider including "Don't know" as a choice.

___ 5.4 Ask respondents to evaluate only salient characteristics.

___ 5.5 Consider asking respondents if they would recommend the product, service, or program to others.

___ 5.6 When determining the content for items in a program evaluation, refer to the services and objectives stated in the proposal for the program.

___ 5.7 Consider asking some open-ended questions.

Chapter 6: Conducting Item Tryouts and an Item Analysis

___ 6.1 Have your items reviewed by others.

___ 6.2 Conduct "think-alouds" with several people.

___ 6.3 Carefully select individuals for think-alouds.

___ 6.4 Consider asking about 10 individuals to write detailed responses on a draft of your questionnaire.

___ 6.5 Ask 25 or more respondents to respond to the questionnaire for an item analysis.

___ 6.6 In the first stage of an item analysis, tally the number of respondents who selected each choice.

___ 6.7 In the second stage of an item analysis, compare the responses of high and low groups on individual items.

Chapter 7: Preparing a Questionnaire for Administration

___ 7.1 Write a descriptive title for the questionnaire.

___ 7.2 Write an introduction to the questionnaire.

___ 7.3 Group the items by content, and provide a subtitle for each group.

___ 7.4 Within each group of items, place items with the same format together.

___ 7.5 At the end of the questionnaire, indicate what respondents should do next.

___ 7.6 Prepare an informed consent form, if needed.

___ 7.7 If the questionnaire will be mailed to respondents, avoid having your correspondence look like junk mail.

___ 7.8 If the questionnaire will be mailed, consider including a token reward.

___ 7.9 If the questionnaire will be mailed, write a follow-up letter.

___ 7.10 If the questionnaire will be administered in person, consider preparing written instructions for the administrator.

Chapter 8: Selecting a Sample of Respondents

___ 8.1 Identify the accessible population.

___ 8.2 Avoid using samples of convenience.

___ 8.3 Simple random sampling is a desirable method of sampling.

___ 8.4 Systematic sampling is an acceptable method of sampling.

___ 8.5 Stratification may reduce sampling errors.

___ 8.6 Consider using random cluster sampling when every member of a population belongs to a group.

___ 8.7 Consider using multistage sampling to select respondents from large populations.

___ 8.8 Consider the importance of getting precise results when determining sample size.

___ 8.9 Remember that using a large sample does not compensate for a bias in sampling.

___ 8.10 Consider sampling nonrespondents to get information on the nature of a bias.

Chapter 9: Preparing Statistical Tables and Figures

___ 9.1 Prepare a table of frequencies.

___ 9.2 Consider calculating percentages and arranging them in a table with the frequencies.

___ 9.3 For nominal data, consider constructing a bar graph.

___ 9.4 Consider preparing a histogram to display a distribution of scores.

___ 9.5 Consider preparing polygons if distributions of scores are to be compared.

Chapter 10: Describing Averages and Variability

___ 10.1 Use the median as the average for ordinal data.

___ 10.2 Consider using the mean as the average for equal interval data.

___ 10.3 Use the median as the average for highly skewed, equal interval data.

___ 10.4 Use the range very sparingly as the measure of variability.

___ 10.5 If the median has been selected as the average, use the interquartile range as the measure of variability.

___ 10.6 If the mean has been selected as the average, use the standard deviation as the measure of variability.

___ 10.7 Keep in mind that the standard deviation has a special relationship to the normal curve that helps in its interpretation.

Chapter 11: Describing Relationships

___ 11.1 For the relationship between two nominal variables, prepare a contingency table.

___ 11.2 When groups have unequal numbers of respondents, include percentages in contingency tables.

___ 11.3 For the relationship between two equal interval variables, compute a correlation coefficient.

___ 11.4 Interpret a Pearson r using the coefficient of determination.

___ 11.5 For the relationship between a nominal variable and an equal interval variable, examine differences among averages.

Chapter 12: Estimating Margins of Error

___ 12.1 It is extremely difficult, and often impossible, to evaluate the effects of a bias in sampling.

___ 12.2 When evaluating a percentage, consider the standard error of a percentage.

___ 12.3 When evaluating a mean, consider the standard error of the mean.

___ 12.4 When evaluating a median, consider the standard error of the median.

___ 12.5 Consider building confidence intervals, especially when comparing two or more groups.

Chapter 13: Writing Reports of Questionnaire Research

___ 13.1 In an informal report, variations in the organization of the report are permitted.

___ 13.2 Academic reports should begin with a formal introduction that cites literature.

___ 13.3 The second section of academic reports should describe the research methods.

___ 13.4 The third section of academic reports should describe the results.

___ 13.5 The last section of academic reports should be a discussion.

___ 13.6 Acknowledge any weakness in your research methodology.

Appendix A

Other Computational Procedures

In this appendix, we will consider how to compute the Pearson correlation coefficient and how to determine the precise 95% margin of error and confidence interval for a mean based on a small sample.

Computation of the Pearson Correlation Coefficient

If you have a large number of respondents, you will undoubtedly want to use a computer program to calculate the Pearson correlation coefficient, whose symbol is r. For those of you who wish to try your hand at it using a calculator, we will consider the following example in which attitudes toward illegal drugs will be correlated with respect for authority. To compute the Pearson r, first set up a worktable such as that shown in Table A.1. Notice that there are two scores per person, which are listed in columns 2 and 3. To get column 4, simply square the values in column 2 (for example, 5 x 5 = 25 for Phil). To get column 5, simply square the values in column 3 (for example, 0 x 0 = 0 for Phil). To get column 6, simply multiply the values in column 2 by the values in column 3 (for example, 5 x 0 = 0 for Phil). Then sum columns 2 through 6; the sums are shown in the last row of the worktable.

Table A.1 *Worktable for computing a Pearson r*

Col. 1	Col. 2	Col. 3	Col. 4	Col. 5	Col. 6
Person	Attitude toward drugs	Respect for authority	Col. 2 squared	Col. 3 squared	Col. 2 times Col. 3
Phil	5	0	25	0	0
Bill	7	4	49	16	28
Carol	0	9	0	81	0
Lila	1	7	1	49	7
Frank	4	5	16	25	20
Jackie	2	6	4	36	12
Sum =	19	31	95	207	67

Next enter the *sums* of the columns in the following formula along with N, which is the number of cases. In this case, there are 6 people responding, so $N = 6$.

133

$$r = \frac{N(Col.6) - (Col.2)(Col.3)}{\sqrt{[N(Col.4) - (Col.2)^2][N(Col.5) - (Col3)^2]}}$$

$$r = \frac{6(67) - (19)(31)}{\sqrt{[(6)(95) - 19^2][(6)(207) - 31^2]}}$$

$$r = \frac{402 - 589}{\sqrt{[570 - 361][1242 - 961]}}$$

$$r = \frac{-187}{\sqrt{[209][281]}}$$

$$r = \frac{-187}{\sqrt{58729}} = \frac{-187}{242.340} = -.771 = -.77$$

Thus, we have found that the Pearson r for the relationship between attitude toward illegal drugs and respect for authority equals $-.77$. The fact that it is negative indicates that those who have more positive attitudes toward illegal drugs have less respect for authority.

Determining the 95% Margin of Error and Confidence Interval for a Mean Based on a Small Sample

In Chapter 12, you learned how to compute the 95% margin of error for the mean of a group consisting of 60 or more respondents: Simply multiply the standard error of the mean by 1.96. For technical reasons that are beyond the scope of this book, the multiplier of 1.96 is not precisely correct when using smaller samples; instead, look up the appropriate multiplier in Table A.2. Specifically, look up your sample size in Column 1 to determine the appropriate multiplier in Column 2.

Let's consider this example:
Mean = 28.90
Standard deviation = 5.45
Number of respondents = 22
Standard error of the mean = 1.16, which is also known as the 68% margin of error

Instead of multiplying 1.16 by 1.96 to get the 95% margin of error, we look up the sample size (in this case, 22) in Column 1 of Table A.2. To the right of 22, we find this multiplier: 2.080. Multiplying 1.16 by 2.080, we get a 95% margin of error equal to 2.41. For the 95% confidence interval, we subtract this product from the mean and add it to the mean as follows:

$$28.90 - 2.41 = 26.49$$
$$28.90 + 2.41 = 31.31$$

Thus, the 95% confidence interval ranges from 26.49 to 31.31. We can have 95% confidence that the mean of the entire population from which this sample was drawn at random is between 26.49 and 31.31.

Table A.2   *Multipliers for 95% margins of error for means based on small samples*

Col. 1	Col. 2	Col. 1 (Cont.)	Col. 2 (Cont.)
Number of respondents	Multiplier for 95% confidence	Number of respondents	Multiplier for 95% confidence
2	12.706	18	2.110
3	4.303	19	2.101
4	3.182	20	2.093
5	2.776	21	2.086
6	2.571	22	2.080
7	2.447	23	2.074
8	2.365	24	2.069
9	2.306	25	2.064
10	2.262	26	2.060
11	2.228	27	2.056
12	2.201	28	2.052
13	2.179	29	2.048
14	2.160	30	2.045
15	2.145	40	2.021
16	2.131	60	2.000
17	2.120		

Note: For numbers of cases between n of 30 and n of 40 and for numbers of cases between n of 40 and n of 60, you may use the nearest value; to be conservative, use the lower value. Values shown for ns of 40 and 60 are close approximations. This table has been adapted from a standard t table for a two-tailed test. Specifically, values of df have been replaced with values of n, and the values of the multipliers have each been shifted accordingly.

Appendix B

Introduction to Statistical Significance

In Chapter 12, you learned how to compare confidence intervals to determine whether a difference is reliable in light of the potential errors created by random sampling. Comparing confidence intervals is an informal significance test.

In this appendix, you will learn the basic concepts underlying formal significance testing as well as when to apply some of the most common tests. Unfortunately, it is beyond the scope of this book to delve into the theory underlying formal significance testing and the related computational mechanics.

Formal significance testing begins with the *null hypothesis*. This is a statistical hypothesis that asserts that any differences we observe when studying random samples are the result of random (chance) errors created by the random sampling. For example, suppose you asked a random sample of men in some population and a random sample of women from the same population whether they support legalizing physician-assisted suicide for the terminally ill and found that 51% of the women supported it while only 48% of the men supported it. At first, you might be tempted to report that women are more supportive of this proposition than men. However, the null hypothesis warns us that the 3-percentage-point difference between women and men may have resulted solely from sampling errors. In other words, there may be no difference between men and women in the population — we may have found a difference because we administered our questionnaire to only these two particular samples.

Of course, it is also possible that the men and women in the population are truly different in their opinion on physician-assisted suicide, and the population difference is responsible for the difference between the percentages for the two samples. In other words, the samples may accurately reflect the gender difference between the populations. This possibility is called an *alternative hypothesis* (that is, an alternative to the null hypothesis).

Which hypothesis is correct? It turns out that the only way to answer this question is to test the null hypothesis. If the test indicates that we may reject the null hypothesis, then we will be left with only the alternative hypothesis as an explanation. When we reject the null hypothesis, we say that we have identified a *reliable* difference — one we can rely on because it probably is not just an artifact of random errors.

Through a set of computational procedures that are beyond the scope of this book, a significance test results in a *probability that the null hypothesis is true*. The symbol for this probability is *p*. By conventional standards, when the

136

probability is as low or lower than 5 in 100, we reject the null hypothesis. (Note that a low probability means it is unlikely that the null hypothesis is true. If something is *unlikely* to be true, we reject it as a possibility.)

The formal term that researchers use when discussing the rejection of the null hypothesis is *statistical significance*. For example, the following two statements might appear in a research report:

"The difference between the means of the liberals and conservatives is statistically significant ($p < .05$)."

"The difference between the means for the men and women is not statistically significant ($p > .05$)."

The first statement says that the probability that the null hypothesis is true is less than ($<$) 5 in 100; thus, the null hypothesis is rejected and the difference is declared to be statistically significant. The second statement says that the probability that the null hypothesis is true is greater than ($>$) 5 in 100; thus, the null hypothesis is *not* rejected, and the difference is *not statistically significant*.

In other words, significance tests are helping us make decisions based on the odds that something is true. We all do this in everyday life. For instance, when you prepare to cross a busy street, you look at oncoming cars to judge their speed and distance to see if it is safe to cross. If you decide that there is a *low probability* that you will be able to cross the street safely, you *reject* the hypothesis that it is safe to cross the street.

In Table B.1 are the names of some of the most popular basic tests and when they can be used. Keep in mind that all significance tests result in a probability on the truth of a null hypothesis.

Table B.1   *Popular basic significance tests*

Name of test	Purpose
z test and *t* test	To compare two means; to compare two Pearson correlation coefficients.
Analysis of variance (ANOVA)	To compare two or more means.
Mann-Whitney *U* test	To compare two medians.[1]
Chi square test	To compare two or more percentages.[2]

[1] Technically, this is a test of distributions. If the distributions are significantly different, it is safe to assume that the medians are significantly different.

[2] Chi square calculations are performed on frequencies, but the results apply to the percentages derived from the frequencies.

Appendix C

Table of Random Numbers

Row #																		
1	2	1	0		4	9	8		0	8	8		8	0	6		9	2	4		8	2	6
2	0	7	3		0	2	9		4	8	2		7	8	9		8	9	2		9	7	1
3	4	4	9		0	0	2		8	6	2		6	7	7		7	3	1		2	5	1
4	7	3	2		1	1	2		0	7	7		6	0	3		8	3	4		7	8	1
5	3	3	2		5	8	3		1	7	0		1	4	0		7	8	9		3	7	7
6	6	1	2		0	5	7		2	4	4		0	0	6		3	0	2		8	0	7
7	7	0	9		3	3	3		7	4	0		4	8	8		9	3	5		8	0	5
8	7	5	1		9	0	9		1	5	2		6	5	0		9	0	3		5	8	8
9	3	5	6		9	6	5		0	1	9		4	6	6		7	5	6		8	3	1
10	8	5	0		3	9	4		3	4	0		6	5	1		7	4	4		6	2	7
11	0	5	9		6	8	7		4	8	1		5	5	0		5	1	7		1	5	8
12	7	6	2		2	6	9		6	1	9		7	1	1		4	7	1		6	2	0
13	3	8	4		7	8	9		8	2	2		1	6	3		8	7	0		4	6	1
14	1	9	1		8	4	5		6	1	8		1	2	4		4	4	2		7	3	4
15	1	5	3		6	7	6		1	8	4		3	1	8		8	7	7		6	0	4
16	0	5	5		3	6	0		7	1	3		8	1	4		6	7	0		4	3	5
17	2	2	3		8	6	0		9	1	9		0	4	4		7	6	8		1	5	1
18	2	3	3		2	5	5		7	6	9		4	9	7		1	3	7		9	3	8
19	8	5	5		0	5	3		7	8	5		4	5	1		6	0	4		8	9	1
20	0	6	1		1	3	4		8	6	4		3	2	9		4	3	8		7	4	1
21	9	1	1		8	2	9		0	6	9		6	9	4		2	9	9		0	6	0
22	3	7	8		0	6	3		7	1	2		6	5	2		7	6	5		6	5	1
23	5	3	0		5	1	2		1	0	9		1	3	7		5	6	1		2	5	0
24	7	2	4		8	6	7		9	3	8		7	6	0		9	1	6		5	7	8
25	0	9	1		6	7	0		3	8	0		9	1	5		4	2	3		2	4	5
26	3	8	1		4	3	7		9	2	4		5	1	2		8	7	7		4	1	3

Appendix D

Editor's Note: The following is the *first draft* of a questionnaire designed to measure attitudes toward statistics. Its purpose is to assess the attitudes of students who are near the end of their first course in statistics. The first five questions (1–5) are designed to measure students' *feelings* toward statistics, the next five (6–10) are designed to measure students' *actions* that may reveal their attitudes, and the next five (11–15) are designed to measure *perceived usefulness of statistics*.

Sample Questionnaire:

Attitudes Toward Statistics Questionnaire

Directions: This questionnaire asks for your opinions on statistics. Since an opinion is neither right nor wrong, there are no right or wrong answers. Your responses will be anonymous. Do *not* put your name on this sheet. Your honest reactions will be appreciated.

Answer each of the following items by placing a check in the box to the left of the choice that best represents your opinion. The choices are:

SA = Strongly Agree   A = Agree   N = Neutral   D = Disagree   SD = Strongly Disagree

Mark only one choice per item. Please respond to all items!!

	SA	A	N	D	SD
1. I get a feeling of malaise when I think about statistics.	☐ SA	☐ A	☐ N	☐ D	☐ SD
2. Statistics is one of my least favorite subjects.	☐ SA	☐ A	☐ N	☐ D	☐ SD
3. Coming to statistics class makes me anxious.	☐ SA	☐ A	☐ N	☐ D	☐ SD
4. I will be very glad when my statistics class is over.	☐ SA	☐ A	☐ N	☐ D	☐ SD
5. Statistics is a very boring field.	☐ SA	☐ A	☐ N	☐ D	☐ SD
6. I have told my friends that statistics is interesting.	☐ SA	☐ A	☐ N	☐ D	☐ SD
7. I will avoid taking additional statistics courses.	☐ SA	☐ A	☐ N	☐ D	☐ SD
8. I do my best to attend all my statistics classes.	☐ SA	☐ A	☐ N	☐ D	☐ SD
9. I can do my statistics homework quickly.	☐ SA	☐ A	☐ N	☐ D	☐ SD
10. I often complain about my statistics course.	☐ SA	☐ A	☐ N	☐ D	☐ SD
11. Statistics will be useful in my future profession.	☐ SA	☐ A	☐ N	☐ D	☐ SD
12. My statistics course will be useful in future courses that I take.	☐ SA	☐ A	☐ N	☐ D	☐ SD
13. Taking statistics will help get me into graduate school.	☐ SA	☐ A	☐ N	☐ D	☐ SD
14. Statistics is irrelevant to my future goals.	☐ SA	☐ A	☐ N	☐ D	☐ SD
15. Statistics has many useful applications in everyday life as well as in future schooling.	☐ SA	☐ A	☐ N	☐ D	☐ SD

Continued on next page.

16. In your own words, describe your feelings toward statistics on the lines below. Attach additional sheets of paper if necessary.

_____
_____
_____
_____
_____
_____
_____
_____
_____
_____
_____
_____
_____

17. What one thing did you like *most* and like *least* about your statistics class?

_____
_____
_____
_____

18. Your age?
   ☐ Under 18   ☐ 19–20   ☐ 21–22   ☐ 23–24   ☐ 25–27   ☐ 28–30

19. Your major? _____

20. Gender?
   ☐ Male   ☐ Female

21. Why did you enroll in this statistics course?
   ☐ It was a required course in my major.
   ☐ Because I plan to attend graduate school.
   ☐ Because of personal interest.

22. Other comments:

When you have answered all the questions, fold your questionnaire in half and place it in the box at the front of the classroom. Thank you!

Appendix E

Editor's Note: The following is the *first draft* of a questionnaire. Its purpose is to collect data for a comprehensive evaluation of a campus bookstore. This questionnaire is presented here for you to critique after you have worked through Chapters 1–5 and 7. In addition, your instructor may ask you to pilot test this questionnaire (see Chapter 6).

Sample Questionnaire:

Campus Bookstore Evaluation

Would you please take a few minutes to answer the questions on this survey? Your responses will provide feedback that we will share with the bookstore's management so they can serve you better in the future. Please return this questionnaire in the attached business reply envelope.

> Thank you,
> Paula Z. Cizmare
> Graduate Student, Library Sciences

1. How many purchases did you make at the campus bookstore during the previous semester?
   ☐ None   ☐ 1-3   ☐ 4-5   ☐ 6-8   ☐ 9+

2. What types of purchases did you make? (Check all that apply.)
   ☐ Textbooks
   ☐ Trade books
   ☐ Writing supplies
   ☐ Computer software
   ☐ Computer hardware
   ☐ School spirit items (items with college logos)

3. Were all of the required books for your classes in stock during the first week of the semester?
   ☐ Yes   ☐ No
   If no, how many days did you have to wait until they were in stock? ____

4. How would you rate the overall service you received during the first week of the semester?
   ☐ Excellent   ☐ Good   ☐ Fair   ☐ Poor   ☐ Don't know

Continued on next page.

5. How would you rate the overall service you received during subsequent weeks of the semester?
☐ Excellent   ☐ Good   ☐ Fair   ☐ Poor   ☐ Don't know

6. Did you telephone the bookstore for information during the semester?
☐ Yes   ☐ No
If yes, how would you rate the service you received by telephone?
☐ Excellent   ☐ Good   ☐ Fair   ☐ Poor   ☐ Don't know

7. Are there items that the bookstore does not currently sell that you would like to be able to purchase there?
☐ Yes   ☐ No
If yes, please name the items: _____

8. How would you rate the bookstore's physical layout?
☐ Excellent   ☐ Good   ☐ Fair   ☐ Poor   ☐ Don't know

9. How would you rate the bookstore's ambience (lighting, color, etc.)?
☐ Excellent   ☐ Good   ☐ Fair   ☐ Poor   ☐ Don't know

10. What one feature of the bookstore do you like the *best*?

_____

11. What one feature of the bookstore do you like the *least*?

_____

12. What one thing could the bookstore management do that would most increase your satisfaction?

_____

13. ABOUT YOU
Your name: _____

Your major: _____

Year in school (e.g., freshman): _____

Your daytime telephone number: _____

Your age: _____

Appendix F

Questions on Race Used in the 2000 Census

The following questions regarding race were posed on the 2000 Census.

→ **NOTE: Please answer BOTH Questions 7 and 8.**

7. Is Person 1 Spanish/Hispanic/Latino? Mark ⊠ the **"No"**
box if **not** Spanish/Hispanic/Latino.

☐ **No,** not Spanish/Hispanic/Latino   ☐ Yes, Puerto Rican

☐ Yes, Mexican, Mexican Am., Chicano   ☐ Yes, Cuban

☐ Yes, other Spanish/Hispanic/Latino – *Print group.*

8. What is Person 1's race? Mark ⊠ **one or more races** to
indicate what this person considers himself/herself to be.

☐ White

☐ Black, African Am., or Negro

☐ American Indian or Alaska Native – *Print name of enrolled or principal tribe.*

☐ Asian Indian   ☐ Japanese   ☐ Native Hawaiian

☐ Chinese   ☐ Korean   ☐ Guamanian or Chamorro

☐ Filipino   ☐ Vietnamese   ☐ Samoan

☐ Other Asian – *Print race.*   ☐ Other Pacific Islander – *Print race.*

☐ Some other race. – *Print race.*

Notes: